R.I.P.

THE KING AND I
Travels in Tigerland

Prerna Singh Bindra

Rupa & Co

Copyright © Prerna Singh Bindra 2006

Published 2006 by

Rupa & Co

7/16, Ansari Road, Daryaganj
New Delhi-110002

Sales Centres:
Allahabad Bangalore Chandigarh
Chennai Hyderabad Jaipur Kathmandu
Kolkata Mumbai Pune

All rights reserved.
No part of this publication may be reproduced, stored in retrieval system, or transmitted, in any form or by any means, electronic, mechanical, photocopying, recording or otherwise, without the prior permission of the publishers.

Designed by Bikram Grewal and Prerna Singh Bindra

Some of these chapters appeared in different forms in *Darpan* and *The Pioneer*. The author would like to express her thanks to them.

Printed in India by
Gopsons Paper Ltd.
A-14, Sector 60, Noida-201301

Contents

Introduction	6
Ranthambhore	12
Rajaji	24
Dudhwa	32
Namdapha	44
Sundarbans	54
Pench/Kanha	66
Manas	78
Gir	90
Melghat	98
Bandipur	106
Leopard	120
Palamau	132
Snow Leopard	144
Panna	156
Kaziranga	166
Nilgiri Foothills	178
Bandhavgarh	186
Cheetah	198
Corbett Country	206
Sariska	220
Tiger: A Status Report	232

Introduction

On the Trail of India's Big Cats

Paradoxically, two of the most profound images of the Royal Bengal Tiger I carry are of ones I haven't seen. No dramatic meetings, no life and death situations, no deadly charges but encounters so potent that they encapsulate the future of this charismatic and endangered species. Bleak but not without hope. Powerful yet helpless. Numerous yet alone.

It was a bitterly cold night at Betla. I sought refuge in the kitchen of the resthouse in Jharkhand's only tiger reserve, Palamau, huddled close to the fire in the company of forest guards and trackers. The night was silent, except for the sounds of the fire, which hissed and cackled as we fed the flames. Then the still night air broke: *Aaaaaummm, aaaauummm...* a soft moan rolling over the hills and through the forest. It was a tigress calling for her mate. Continual. Persistent. Desperate. We listened, unable to delight in the sign of the animal, distressed by the doomed fate of Betla's only tigress, Rani. She was the queen of her forest, but her kingdom was an island. There were no males to woo, tease, tantalise and mate. She was six, if nature had her way, she would have been a mother by now, preparing to let go of her first litter. It was not to be, and her entreaties ended with a frustrated growl. Rani faded away, condemned to eternal solitude. With her will die the last tiger of Betla, the best-protected area of a fragmented Palamau.

Rani represents the biggest fear for the tiger, as they are pushed further and further into isolated pockets, inbreeding and shrinking into small, threatened populations. I remember another time, another place. I was in the Chilla range in the Rajaji National Park, not a designated tiger reserve, but definitely its domain. Or at least it was, till the Van Gujjars, a nomadic tribe took over and made the range their permanent abode. I took in the devastation – the streams had been reduced to a toxic trickle, trees were hacked to stumps, the grass worn out and eaten by livestock. Rubbish carpeted the forest floor and no wild animal dared venture into this human habitat. Then, after a long patient process, the Gujjars were rehabilitated. I walked through the same land a year later. Yesterday's scars had been healed by nature and my eyes met a rejuvenated forest; streams gushed with clear water, leafy trees hosted screeching parakeets, cheetal munched on tall grasses. Prospective meal had lured the carnivore; I traced the pugmarks of a tigress with tinier prints dutifully following behind. A mother with cubs. The tiger had reclaimed its home.

The KING and I

The animal that inspired the world's biggest conservation initiative, Project Tiger, had sent a simple message: Leave me and my home alone and I will thrive.

India has the maximum number of tigers; it is here that hope for their future reigns. India is also home to more than a billion people, which leaves little room for big, predatory carnivores already decimated by the gun. Hope is fading, though, like the tiger, like its forests.

Does the *Panthera tigris tigris* have a future? Has Project Tiger played a role in its continued, if precarious, survival? These are questions that the book will attempt to deal with. It is primarily a travelogue in tiger country. It is my ever so humble tribute to the tiger and the other big cats, in whose domain I have found much joy and peace. It expresses my profound fear for India's wild denizens. My worry for their future.

There is no species on earth that has fascinated man more than the tiger. They first appeared in human art in the 5,000-year-old seals from the Harappan civilisation in the Indus valley. There is an interesting seal, dating back to that time, that depicts a distinctly unhappy man sitting on a tree, apparently pleading with a tiger waiting for him below, presumably for a meal!

The tiger is intrinsic to Asian culture and religion; it is the guardian of the forest, the supreme protector and the symbol of fertility and virility. In India, the tiger is the hallowed steed of Goddess Durga; in Tibet, the tiger averts evil and among the Warli tribe in the Konkan region it is the greatest of all Gods. So strong is the veneration for the tiger that even man-eaters, while feared, are not really hated. I remember a film that showed the slain body

Leopard

Introduction

of a man-eater being carried through a village. There were no cries of triumph and joy, just a deep reverence by the people the tiger had terrorised, and indeed preyed upon. The villagers, including a survivor, showered flowers on the dead tiger and touched its feet reverently.

There is no such devotion for the leopard, the other big cat that lives in the shadow of the tiger, both in the jungle and the people's conscience. I was almost a witness – I arrived a little too late – to a mob which had beaten and stoned a cornered leopard to death. This was in a tiny village in Uttaranchal and the victim was a suspected man-eater. It was the second leopard the village had killed in a row. The crowd was upbeat, relieved at bringing to justice the beast, which had ravaged three of their children in as many months. The leopard has withstood many such batterings all across the country as it has become the cornerstone of man-animal conflict. India's spotted predator inhabits almost all kinds of habitats, from dense jungles to sparse deserts, snowy hills to riverine islands. The leopard is a much-maligned animal. In the forest, where prey is sufficient, it rarely attacks man, proving it is only stress of circumstances that forces it to stray into human territory and attack man. A wild leopard is a shy, elusive creature that prefers to steer clear of humans. Those who know the leopard say that pound for pound its power is unmatched, that it is agile and adaptable. It can live like a pauper or a king, depending on the circumstances.

If the leopard has its pugmark in most of India, the Asiatic Lion is confined to just over 800 square kilometres in Gir, a national park in Gujarat. The lion is special to me; it was the first big cat I ever glimpsed, as a child of seven hiding behind my mother's sari, not twenty

Snow Leopard

The KING and I

feet away from a sleeping lion. There were no barriers between us, no borders, not even the reassuring safety of a nearby jeep. The cat reposed in feline slumber and I was lulled into mistaking the sleeping lion as nothing more than a large pussycat. I ventured closer and the lion snapped to attention, throwing back its mane to deliver a terrifying roar, its jaws opening wide to reveal sharp, powerful canines, its eyes narrowing into cold gold slits. It was a warning: Do not invade my territory. I learnt an early lesson: Let sleeping lions lie.

My last big cat is the most beautiful, yes, even more so than the tiger. And so mysterious and secretive that the Snow Leopard has earned itself the title of the 'grey ghost of the mountains'. My foray into their lofty territory was brief, my acquaintance so fleeting that it seemed a glorious dream.

The Clouded Leopard is the smallest of the big cats and incredibly lovely. Its unique coat is its enemy, they are killed for their fur which commands a high price in the illegal skin market. It is a secretive cat, a rare sight in the wild. Its numbers are unknown, but definitely small. Though I have ventured into its habitat in Namdapha in the northeast, the arboreal creature escaped me.

While the book celebrates India's four big cats, it mourns the loss of another. The Cheetah, the world's fastest animal is extinct in India. Its employ as a hunter for blackbuck, trophy hunting and a diminishing habitat, scripted the cheetah's epitaph. The year 1947 was a significant one for India; she won independence and was cruelly cut into two in a partition

Lioness

Introduction

Clouded Leopard

bathed in blood. The year was also significant from the natural history point of view. India shot to death the last cheetah; three males were killed in the native state of Korea in Madhya Pradesh by the Maharajah of the principality.

This book is about my travels in wild India, in search of elusive big cats. That minuscule portion of this chaotic, wonderful country that is wild. Free and exotic. Untamed and natural. Where time has paused for a break and forgotten to come back. It is Mother Earth before Man. It is where nature's children reside, somehow I find it difficult to imagine *Homo sapiens* as nature's creations – I shudder to think that children repay their eternal debt to Mother by death and destruction.

This is my big cat book, for not only do the animals possess unbeatable charisma, but also the canids represent, in a grand manner, most of India's wild habitats. Big cat country covers the length and breadth of India – vast deserts and snowy peaks, lush evergreen forests and dry scrub habitats, leaving out the beautiful islands of Lakshadweep, Andaman and Nicobar and the Thar desert. The land of the tiger has been an unending discovery of creatures great and small, all equally exciting and deeply enigmatic. From the thrilling encounter with the thought-to-be extinct, decidedly drab Spotted Forest Owlet to the awesome majesty of the Asian Elephant.

Words fall pathetically short to recreate the magic of nature; I can only hope that they convey even a fraction of the joy I feel when I share the territory of the big cats, walking their walk, footprint trailing pugmark.

Born to be King

Ranthambhore, in Rajasthan, almost didn't make it to the list of the nine tiger reserves presented to Prime Minister Indira Gandhi for approval in 1973, but went on to become the most notorious and celebrated park in the country. It was the hunting preserve of the royal house of Jaipur, and you can still see a faded photograph of HRH the Duke of Edinburgh, with his foot resting on a slain tiger, a prize trophy he bagged as late as 1961. Today, Ranthambhore rates high among the best places to see a tiger, and there couldn't be a more beautiful locale to see one. The jungle is verdant and green with golden grasses set against the background of an ancient royal fort. But then, I am prejudiced, for it was here, at Ranthambhore, that I was introduced to the fabled world of tigers.

Bumbooram is my tiger on the wall, the most beautiful animal I never saw. He had his brush with fame when he was alive but it was in his death that he became immortal. He lives in the hearts of those who crossed his regal path. He continues to trouble our collective conscience, a constant reminder of our failure to preserve his kith and kin, of our brutality as a race that we reduce this royal feline to a rug on the floor and his bones into a pill to boost impotent souls.

The truth is that Bumbooram was quite an ordinary animal. As ordinary as this extraordinary animal can be. I am told he was the shy type, keeping a safe distance from the limelight that besiege this popular national park. Where tiger sighting is the order of the day, Bumbooram was a rare encounter, till the most influential man in the world, US President Bill Clinton spotted him.

The KING and I

President Clinton at Ranthambhore

That was March 2000, the President was on an official visit to India, however, seeing the Royal Bengal Tiger was high on his list of priorities. He did. As his convoy rumbled through the forest, an imposing male crossed Clinton's path, converting the US President into a besotted tiger tourist. He junked security pleas, insisting on a picture of himself with the tiger, Bumbooram, in the background. 'A strange name for a tiger, I think,' said the President, and gave him a new one – Boomerang.

Bumbooram

'He was huge, he was beautiful and it was the most memorable moment of my life,' Clinton was to say later, pledging to save this natural heritage. Poachers, however, do not follow presidential diktats.

Boomerang went missing, presumed killed. I broke that story. The cat had not been seen for five months and some poachers had been apprehended with crude traps. Boomerang was dead, though he remained alive in government files. As the world media swooped onto the story, officials were transferred and hell broke loose in parliament. But as it usually happens, the real story remained hidden and the government perpetrated the lie that Boomerang was well and kicking, before he gracefully succumbed to old age. His body, and the fact that he was killed, both got a quiet burial.

I returned later to Ranthambhore, when things had simmered down and other, spicier news had taken over. Death had made Boomerang famous. His portrait, sketched in charcoal and oils, was doing brisk business. 'Buy Bumbooram,' Lokesh, a local artist urged me. I did, and he now hangs on my bedroom wall. He is the first thing I see in the morning and he strengthens my love for his kind, reinforces my commitment to help them survive and increases my resolve not to falter.

Bumbooram was my first big wildlife story; his brutal death was my introduction to the world of tigers. It lured me to his home, Ranthambhore, and for that I am grateful. There can be no better teacher than this incredibly beautiful tiger reserve.

For me, Ranthambhore can never be a story or a travelogue penned in praise of its verdant forest and its charismatic citizens. I can only pay a tribute as a humble but grateful student does to a teacher, as a neophyte does to her master. I was a novice in the ways of the wild when I first went to Ranthambhore many years ago, unaware of nature's rhythms and untutored in the mysterious laws of the jungle. Till then I was a devout citizen of the urban jungle; Ranthambhore bewitched me into being its slave for life.

Jogi Mahal

The KING and I

It is near impossible to list down Ranthambhore's many wonders. But high on the list is Jogi Mahal. Anybody who is anybody has stayed in it: Rajiv and Sonia Gandhi, Amitabh and Jaya Bachchan. By the time I went, Jogi Mahal had closed its hallowed gates to visitors, but I wrangled a few hours in the ancient hunting lodge of the Maharajah of Jaipur sitting astride the Rajbagh Lake. In the backyard stands a banyan tree, so big (it is the second biggest in the country) that it is a tiny town in itself. Parakeets burrowed in hollows, macaques chattered and quarreled, peacocks preened and squirrels busily loaded their larder.

I sat on the verandah overlooking the lotus-filled waters of the Rajbagh Lake. The scene was picture perfect, placid waters disturbed by swimming sambhars, their antlers decorated with green moss, and an occasional bird hitching a free ride. On the banks crocodiles sunned themselves into a stupor. It was so calm and peaceful that you could hear yourself breathe.

Till, the tiger approached stealthy, silently, almost as if he was a ghost; and then exploded into the horizon, all power and all glory. A blur of burnished gold: shattering the calm, scattering the prey, panicking the jungle. Born to be King. Born to rule.

The tiger is undoubtedly the star of India's animal kingdom. And among the stars, the Ranthambhore tiger is arguably the superstar. His exploits have inspired a plethora of books; he has modelled for paintings and he has starred in many a film. Anyone remotely interested in tigers is well acquainted with the reserve's famous felines. There was the flamboyant killer Ghengis, who made hunting in the lake into an art form, charging into the water and swiping the startled deer in one liquid movement; and Noon, his mate, who learnt the tricks of the trade from him but couldn't quite match his skill. There was Machli, star of a BBC film, and First Tiger Boomerang. Now dead.

The KING and I

I saw my first tiger – tigers, rather – in Ranthambhore, an experience so profound that it is etched deep in my mind and heart, forever.

I was seated in an open jeep, patiently waiting for the predator, with Fateh Singh Rathore, the former director of the park, and my tiger teacher. They were around, said Fatji, sniffing the air. He could smell them. He was right.

I sensed, rather than heard, a faint movement in the bushes beside me. A tiger. Gold and black stripes blending perfectly with the scorched yellow grass. On the other side, I saw a tail snapping in the air, irritatingly lashing out at a fly. Another tiger. I sat, spellbound, unbelieving, when a third walked in from the bushes and settled down behind us, so close his coat grazed the jeep. In seconds, the tiger had drifted off to sleep, eyes shut, maned head thrown back carelessly, paws up in the air. A catnap in the truest sense of the word! I was so overwhelmed by the enormity of the moment that I almost stopped being. I felt a faint touch on my arm; Fatji was smiling, pointing in front.

I spotted my fourth tiger of the day walking in from the bushes, crossing our path. Heavy paws padding the earth soundlessly, oddly so for a creature so huge and powerful. She stopped, gave me a piercing look, golden eye locked for a fleeting, arresting moment with my brown one. I could feel her judging us, weighing her options. Apparently, she thought of us as unworthy opponents for she sat down in front of the jeep, never letting down her guard for even a moment. She was the Bakula tigress, mother of three almost full-grown cubs.

I was in Ranthambhore Tiger Reserve, surrounded by four of the most beautiful, charismatic creatures in this world. I was in paradise.

Should I have been scared, hemmed in by all sides by nature's most powerful predator? I wasn't. I just felt blessed. And touched by the trust shown in us humans, even when we had persecuted them ruthlessly. I wanted the moment to last forever, but good times rarely do, and I went away, a firm tiger addict.

I have now seen many more tigers in Ranthambhore. Here, tigers are not mere tigers, they are Bachi, Machli, Nick-Ear, Isabelle, named after a BBC cameraman's daughter. Here, tigers don't just rule their reserve, they dominate community life as well. It is like a well-oiled tiger economy: hotels lure tourists on promised sightings, guides are obsessed with the tiger of the day; who saw it, who didn't, which one was it, and most importantly, where was it. Many local people run a neat little business selling tiger T-shirts, caps, books etc. Local artists have been trained to sketch the tiger and I occasioned on a tiny barbershop bearing a signboard 'Tiger Cut!'

The history and vital statistics of each of the thirty-five odd tigers are well-detailed; each time you see one, the guide will wax eloquent about their antecedents as though extolling a royal lineage. Tiger lore is essential dinner-time conversation, discussing the minutest details of the day: Did you see Jhumri's scat? Do you know Machli killed a sambhar today? To former glory: I saw a tiger kill a croc, *that* was something else. My favourite is a tale that Aditya, a hotelier and keen wildlifer, recounts, of a massive fight between two tigers: Lady of the Lake versus Nick-Ear. 'It is indescribable,' says he. 'The drivers, who see tigers every day, just covered their heads and refused to watch. The best way I can describe the terror of the moment is that I saw langurs fall off the trees. Dead with heart attacks.'

In my most recent visit, I climbed the fort and from my vantage point I spotted the *Panthera tigris tigris*. He was Jhumroo, brother of Jhumri and son of cine star, Machli. Jhumroo made up for his highly unsuitable name by his sheer size and magnificence. I sat for an hour staring as the tiger held audience. Then he moved away, the unchallenged sovereign of the forest.

The KING and I

Ranthambhore is much more than tigers. The beauty is almost surreal, a jungle sometimes lush and green, at other times dry and golden with spectator views, where two mountain ranges, the Aravallis and Vindhayas merge. The jungle is guarded by an ancient fort dating back a thousand years and once the centre of an important Hindu kingdom. The invader Allaudin Khilji defeated Rana Hamir in 1301 A D, forcing his many wives to commit sati. The Rajputs won it back and restored it to its former glory, until Emperor Akbar occupied it again after a forty-day war. The Mughals however returned it and it remained with the Jaipur royal family till 1949, when the states were merged into the Indian Union. Legend has it that the King sent the condemned to this fort. Writes Francois Bernier, the seventeenth century traveller, 'They (the condemned) are for the most part kept here for two months, after which the governor brings them out, places them on top of the wall, and having caused them to drink some milk, casts them down headlong into the rocks beneath'. In the present day, the only gory event here is a leopard condemning a langur to a swift death.

After Ranthambhore, I have visited many forests and seen many a tiger (never enough, though, never enough), each encounter more thrilling than the other. But Ranthambhore is special; it is my proverbial first love. Forever special and forever treasured.

Ranthambhore

There but for the Grace of God go I...

Rajaji National Park is the final vestige of what were once the Terai jungles at the base of the Himalayas. The Shiwalik hills run through the park. These hills have unearthed rich fossil deposits including the remains of prehistoric elephants, like Stegodon ganesa whose tusks extended over ten feet. Today their descendants, roughly about 400 in number survive tenuously in the 820 square kilometres of Rajaji. The park marks the end of their north-western range. There is not a problem that doesn't beset this unfortunate sanctuary: Three burgeoning cities surround it, about 2,000 families and their 15,000 cattle live within its boundaries. National highways and railway lines cut through the forest, a hurdle to the natural behaviour and free movement of animals. But all that survives is beautiful, all the more so for its fragile future.

A visit to the forest does not end when you walk out of the gate or cross the harsh borders that delineate a green haven from urban chaos, peace from turmoil, paradise from reality, wilderness from 'civilisation'. For me the relationship is an abiding one. It lingers after I have been there, seen this, done that. To know a forest is to love it. It brings immense pleasure, but is not without its share of heartache. Elation at the life that nature nurtures, grief for its fragility. Each forest leaves a multitude of impressions, a few imprint themselves in the mind and become symbols, signifying my relationship to the forest. I came back from Rajaji with two distinct images, one fraught with despair, the other a symbol of hope.

Let's give hope a hearing first. Mine is contained in a photograph of a tigress, taken somewhere around midnight by the animal itself, who inadvertently placed her heavy paw on the wire that pulled the shutter of the strategically placed camera trap. She's a healthy female and my gaze travelled over her tawny frame to rest on her teats, swollen and heavy with milk. Nothing earth-shattering, one might think. There are tigers, and there are pregnant tigresses. But not in Chilla. Not at least for the past two decades.

The KING and I

Gujjar and his settlement in Rajaji

Chilla is that rare conservation success story where a jungle ravaged by human pressure has sprung back to life. Chilla, and indeed Rajaji, serve as a classic example of how wildlife issues in India are inevitably linked with people; that habitat and resource competition between man and beast is a volatile problem and that man-animal conflict is the biggest concern in conservation today. I lay claim to no scientific studies, but Chilla taught me that man and beast can not live together in peace. Not in this day and age. That their interests conflicted and if wildlife is to survive, we must grant them a tiny part of our country that they can call their own. Inviolate and sacrosanct.

One of the serious pressures in Rajaji is the presence of Gujjars, though there are conflicting views on this and it has become part of a larger debate on the rights of tribals over forestland, and its implications. Van Gujjars are a nomadic Muslim tribe who have been living in Rajaji for many years. It is believed that they first came to the Terai as part of the dowry of a Kashmiri princess who was married in Sirmour, now part of Himachal Pradesh. In ancient times, Gujjars were nomadic graziers moving their herds above onto the upper Himalayas, giving the Terai forests a chance to rejuvenate in their six-month absence. Loss of pastoral lands and other forces have compelled these Gujjars to make Rajaji their permanent abode. Over the years, their population and livestock has spread and increased, creating immense biotic pressure on the park.

Chilla was one such *dera* or settlement. Gujjars used wood to light their fires, their livestock grazed and wallowed in the waterholes. When fodder became scarce, branches from trees were lopped off to feed the cattle. Populations of both man and animal grew and the settlements spread rapidly like cancer, destroying the wilderness. The forest was dying a slow death, degraded almost beyond redemption. Grasses were trampled and the *nullah* that ran through Chilla had been reduced to a stinking trickle, that no elephant or self-respecting animal would deign to use. Wild animals kept away from the scent of man.

Tigers were at best occasional visitors, none felt safe enough to linger on, mate, and breed. Following a Supreme Court order to rehabilitate the Gujjars from the designated protected area, efforts were made to relocate them. The painful procedure began in 2002 and after a traumatic year, 193 Gujjar families were resettled to a village, Gaindikhatta.

I revisited Chilla a year later. Nature had a chance to heal and I soaked in the wilderness. A Forest Eagle Owl, large and beautifully patterned, peered through its tawny eyes, sambhar placidly munched in the meadow and a Red Junglefowl, gaudy progenitor to the domestic one, emerged through the tall, golden grasses, a jackal in hot pursuit. I narrowly missed the leopard, but that was only because I had stopped to look at an elephant family. Two tiny calves carefully tucked beneath their mama's bulk, an assortment of aunts, an impish older calf whom the matriarch strictly brought to order with a resounding whack of her trunk and a young male whose gleaming white tusks had not quite reached full length. I am not really complaining, but had I arrived a few minutes earlier I would have watched a leopard make its kill. Leap from the squat hillocks to the path below on an unsuspecting peacock. On my way inside I had crossed this alley and delighted at seeing a few males doing their fancy number, swaying their glamorous tails energetically to woo a bride. At least one of them did not live happily ever after. It was a clean kill. Not a drop of blood reddened the earth, one canine sinking into the bird's graceful neck was enough. All that remained were feathers, tiny and scraggly, long and gossamer-like, which littered the floor, carefully removed by the cat for a hygienic meal. The drama had passed me by, but had left signs for the imagination to decipher.

A little deeper in the jungle, I saw other signs. Pugmarks. Bigger than a leopard, smaller than the tiger. One big depression framed by four smaller ones. Not squarish like the males' but tapering down to a 'V' surrounded by a mass of tinier prints. A tigress with her cubs. Probably the camera trapped female I had seen on film. I laughed, then cried, the kind of

Yellow-throated Marten

The KING and I

emotion when happiness takes over. This was a miracle. This was hope. This was a lesson. Leave nature alone. Let the tiger be. Protect it and it will bounce back.

The forest officer who accompanied me searched his memory, and his records, for a breeding tigress in this section of the park. And failed. Chilla was nurturing a new generation of tigers after twenty years. It is a strong indicator of a healthy eco-system, for a tigress chooses her nursery only where there is plenty of prey at hand. Prey will thrive if the grasses and foliage do.

My joy is adulterated though; I spent my time in Rajaji relentlessly driving through the park, entering from the Mohand gate, through to Dholkhand, Beribarra, Kansrao and Motichur with brief stops at forest resthouses, built by the British for the weary forester. It's a lovely forest, alive and dense, but pillaged by man and haphazard development.

The image that comes to mind is of a patchwork forest, bits of green interspersed with jungles decayed by human habitation, with roads and railway lines slashing through, fraying the fabric even further. Three highways, a railway line and a canal crisscross through the park, which is encircled by three big cities – Dehradun, the capital of Uttaranchal and two major religious centres, Haridwar and Rishikesh.

Let's take the Kansrao range as an example. It is good, viable wild habitat, if you close your eyes – and ears – to the railway line behind the ancient forest resthouse and the trains thundering through it. Nek Mohammed is a Gujjar employed as caretaker of the resthouse;

he doubles up as guide and beat guard. The resthouse is over a hundred years old. It has now acquired a hideous shade of green, though it still manages to retain much of its charm. Primarily, old cloth *punkhas* that were relentlessly pulled by retainers to stir up fresh air for the sahibs. We settle down for a meal. Nek Mohammed has a repertoire of jungle tales. He tells us of a *makhna* (a tuskless male elephant) who has with alarming regularity knocked down the doors, more often than not when an official drops by.

Most of his stories are tragic. He remembers with horror the day, some three years ago, when a speeding train ran down two females and a calf. Probably, the baby was stuck in the tracks and its mother with another female had tried frantically to pull it out. They died in the attempt. An orphan at the Chilla Elephant Camp, Raja, is the victim of yet another gory accident. That was in 1991 and Raja, then unnamed and still wild, was standing in the tracks, rendered inert by the terrifying and unfamiliar rumble. His mother and another elephant came to his rescue. The calf was pushed off the track, but the females could not get away, the Mussorie Express was too fast and the embankment impeded swift escape. The elephants died, but the tiny, bewildered baby refused to leave its dead mother's side, till a team of foresters, wildlifers, scientists and vets pried him away, not without some difficulty.

The depression lifts when I drive through the Kansrao range. It is lush green, its tall trees and riot of creepers and foliage reminiscent of an evergreen forest. It's a fertile land, harbouring density and diversity of wildlife. The Pied Hornbill, that rare, beautiful bird

The KING and I

Red Junglefowl

Goral

distinguishable by its outlandish 'double' beak becomes a common sight. Cheetal, barking deer, sambhar, wild boar – I sight all of these. A tusker, initially placid, encourages me to inch the jeep a little closer. He is behind a tree, tusks sticking out from the girth of the trunk. I press the shutter to capture the memory of a tusker, up close, when he burst forth, tail stiffly perked up, ears spread wide, trunk held high, trumpeting loudly and surprisingly fast for his bulk. I run. As in the jeep runs. It is only when we are at a safe distance that the tusker calms down. I am told that the elephants here have a vile temper, so stressed are they by a compressed, fragmented habitat. Heavily trafficked roads that hinder their ancient migratory paths, trains that mow them down, people who drive them away and kill when they venture into villages that the pachyderms instinctively know as forests.

My train of thought is interrupted by a frenzy of birdcalls. Not the usual lilting song, but fraught with panic. Undoubtedly prompted by a predator on the prowl. The cause of worry is an ash-golden creature; pointed face, bushy tail stretching longer than the body. The aforesaid creature, a Yellow-throated Marten is an efficient, cunning hunter least fussy about its diet. It will eat eggs, fowl, birds, squirrels, rats, moles and will even take on the young of deer. One of those fascinating animals one knows little about and eclipsed by mega fauna like the tiger.

As we move towards Satyanarayan, the jungle thins out and concrete takes over. A cluster of *pukka* houses, offices and even a real estate agent has intruded into the forest. Though not strictly within the National Park they sit in the midst of the elephant corridor and are slowly edging inside. I turn back, unprepared to be confronted by yet another problematic issue.

Rajaji leaves me confused. If it enamours, it also depresses, to twist an adage, each silver lining here is accompanied by a cloud. If there was ecstasy at seeing Goral walking up a steep hill, there was sorrow at herds of cattle competitively mincing away at the grasses. If there was fear from the elephant that charged at our panicked vehicle, there was terror at the railway tracks that cut through the heart of the reserve. If there was joy on spotting the rare tusker, cold terror gripped the heart that poachers with an evil eye on the tusks were not far, either.

Even then, I wish the story had ended there. And though I always hunger for a glimpse of wildlife, I did not need the grand finale that I was confronted with. My second lasting impression of Rajaji, a stark contrast to the happy family portrait of the tigers. Initially it appeared to be a dull, grey bulk, then the silhouette of a massive tusker took shape, its gleaming white tusks contrasting the night. It stood in the middle of a concrete road, in this strip of development with its fragmented, broken home on both sides. Beyond it, less than a kilometre away, glittered the lights of the holy city of Haridwar.

Mighty and powerful though it seemed, the elephant appeared confused, stumbling without the grace characteristic of its kind, through the maze of panicked vehicles. What future did it have, thrown into direct confrontation with man? Cursed with teeth worth more than their weight in gold. Rajaji has had its share of poaching problems, and Haridwar, despite its sacred tag is well-established as an illegal centre for trade in animal products.

Today, providence was kind, and the tusker disappeared into the jungles of Rajaji National Park. Like the tigers of Chilla, it had a second, precarious lease of life.
There but for the grace of god go I…

Camera-trapped pregnant tigeress at Chilla

Letter From Tiger Haven

Dudhwa Tiger Reserve in Uttar Pradesh, barely a step away from the Nepal border, plays host to two living legends — the Greater One Horned Rhinoceros and India's original 'Tigerwallah' Billy Arjan Singh. Both belong to the mammalian genre, are deceptively placid but equally temperamental. The similarity ends there, the Rhinoceros unicornis *is ancient, a relic of five million years of evolution, the latter a product of the erstwhile royal house of Kapurthala, is a little bent with age, disdains his false teeth yet is afire with purpose. What follows is a letter from Tiger Haven, home to Billy and once a sanctuary to his assorted wild menagerie of tigers and leopards.*

The KING and I

Dear Reader

I count myself fortunate to write this from Tiger Haven. This house set in lush green jungle beside two rivers, Soheli and the deceptively docile Neora, is more receptive to guests of the four-legged kind. It is the home of 'Honourary Tiger' Billy Arjan Singh since 1959.

A disillusioned Billy was seeking solitude, a sanctuary from people and civilisation. He found Tiger Haven.

The space I now occupy was once Tara's domain. Billy's Tara, a captive, zoo-born tigress, nurtured by humans, later released in the wild. Then, there was Prince, an orphaned leopard cub, later followed by Harriet and Juliet, not prim English Misses as their names suggest but two leopards gifted to Billy as cubs by then Prime Minister Indira Gandhi.

I knew Billy as a child, through his books. A member of the erstwhile royal family of Kapurthala, one-time hunter, architect of Dudhwa, foster mother to tiger and leopards. Billy, and his life, had me enthralled. I absorbed with fascination the antics of Tara, the only captive born tigress to be released in the wild, and — foolishly — determined to do the same.

And here I was, some twenty years later, in his living room, surrounded by images of a glorious wild past. Never before have I wished that I was older, my hair a little grayer, my skin withered, to enable me fit into the fading black and white memories framed on the walls. They seem too fantastic to be real, except that the photographs present hard evidence of Billy's extraordinary life. In one Billy is caught in a fierce bear hug with Tara and I wonder how it must be to win the trust of this efficient carnivore. There are others. Billy holding a leopard by its tail, Harriet grooming her human friend, Billy on a stroll followed by his menagerie — leopards, wolves and dog.

My favourite is a series of pictures of Tara, Prince and Elie at play with the joyful abandon of children. Tiger, leopard and mongrel locked not in combat but in playful tussle.

On my first night Billy urges me to watch *The Leopard who Changed its Spots*, a film on his beloved leopard Harriet. When I insist that he give me company, Billy is disdainful. 'I have lived it,' he reasons, 'and seen the film a hundred times over.' But as the reel starts whirring and a beautiful spotted cat stalks the screen, Billy watches raptly. He is seated next to me. And he is on the screen.

In bounds the leopard and leaps on Billy's back with restrained power. They rub their heads together, in the manner of cats, before settling down quietly. The film is seemingly make-believe, a fantastic record of a unique relationship, a romance of man and his leopard, and of his quest to give back to the beleaguered beast its wild home. Harriet fulfills Billy's dream, mating with a wild leopard, and adding to their falling numbers. In the monsoons, when the Neora swallows the jungle she gets the cub to her haven, Billy's home. Once the waters recede, she returns to the forest, but before the final wrench she tours Tiger Haven, cub tenderly held in her mouth, as though bidding farewell… There isn't a dry eye in the audience. Including Billy's.

The leopards inspired Billy to take on a zoo-bred tigress, nurture the cub and release it in Dudhwa. In this he had the support of Prime Minister Indira Gandhi. Tara lived a full life in the wild, giving birth to cubs, though controversy stalks her life. Detractors accused her of contaminating the 'pure bred' Royal Bengal Tigers as she was of Siberian strain. Billy disagrees. 'Inbreeding is more of a problem rather than rallying about mixed blood,' roars

Harriet

The KING and I

Billy. It was worse than a mere matter of genetics. Tara was accused of being a man-eater and a former park tiger claimed to have killed her. Billy doesn't agree, stubbornly believing in the tiger he loved, using logic, and DNA testing to back his claim. Her proximity to man did not make Tara a man-eater. Tara lived a full life, giving to the jungle a whole new generation of tigers. Sentimental certainly, partial maybe, but I am with Billy in this story.

That's the past, but the good old days are not quite gone. My room has a huge square window, that frames an incredible view. It overlooks the Soheli and I can sit there for hours watching a Pied Kingfisher intently peer for his food, aim, then swoop into the waters below. There is the occasional crocodile, sunning itself on the bank, its jaws wide open for any unsuspecting morsel that happens his way.

Top: Billy with Harriet; above: Prince and Elie

Tara

A raucous peacock suffering from an identity crisis renders the morning alarm. Moti imagines himself a hen, he is among a succession of peacocks reared by hens from abandoned eggs discovered by Billy. Moti eyes me pass and throws open his brilliant tail, swaying and dancing in delight. I am delighted though a little bewildered by his attentions, till I am assured that the peacock woos any stimuli – people and cars included – but not a peahen. Another guest of the avian variety is the White-breasted Water Hen, which joins us for breakfast, lunch and tea by politely tapping at the glass window for her share of the repast.

Though I do not sport a striped or spotted coat and lack the tenacity to roar, I am made welcome provided I follow the rules of the household. You could set your clock by mealtimes here, but so caring is the regimented hand, and so peaceful the environs, that I succumb happily. Tiger Haven, and its assorted residents, have seduced me, so much so that Dudhwa Tiger Reserve almost becomes incidental to my visit. Except for the one trip in an open jeep with Billy at the wheel. Our most deadly encounter is not with a beast but people loaded in a truck hurtling at breakneck speed in the heart of the reserve. Billy stops the vehicle. He appears frail, slightly bent with age but there nothing feeble in his stride or in the roar he emits, 'This is the tiger's reserve. What are you doing here?' He cares not that he is a man past eighty, or that the truck is spilling over with drunken louts. He is 'Tigerman' Billy, defending the tiger's fiefdom. Wielding his walking-stick, he snatches the key from the stunned driver, gets back in his vehicle and hands the key to the forest *chowki* nearby. 'Let them rot here through the night before turning them to the police,' he fumes.

Billy is raging, but the tranquility of the jungle soothes him. Enjoy Dudhwa while it lasts, he advises, enjoy the forest, before we, the people, destroy it. We drive to the rhino area. The

The KING and I

advent of the Great One-horned Rhinoceros here makes for an interesting story. Once upon a time rhinos flourished in these Terai plains. There is nothing new in the story of their local extinction. Man came, set up house, ploughed fields, made roads, established factories, destroyed the jungle and the rhino lost its home. Perhaps to atone his sins of the past, or to give the rhino an alternative home, aside from Kaziranga in Assam, man invited this ancient species back to Dudhwa. Two male rhinos were translocated from Assam, and to insure future progeny five brides were imported from Nepal. They settled into their new home, multiplying to a present population of eighteen.

I have the good fortune of seeing Banke, one of the originals from Assam, 100 pounds heavier than an average rhino. Naseem, a guide who has accompanied us, is full of Banke stories. Banke is aggressive by nature, and an irrepressible Casanova. The other male rhinos live in terror of Banke as he fiercely guards over his harem of a dozen females. Woe betide any male with evil intentions towards the women, Banke wants them all. Need I add that all the young rhinos here owe their parentage to Banke.

Harriet and Juliette

The KING and I

Billy Arjan Singh

We head back home, delighted to see the rhino, aggrieved to have not seen even the trace of a tiger.

At the crack of dawn, I take a short walk upstream, armed with nothing but a stick. I have no fiery encounters with big cats to recount but it is clear that the jungle has been extremely busy in the hours gone by. Huge imprints on the sand relay the news that elephants are here and have preceded towards Soheli for a drink and bath. These elephants are temporary visitors from Nepal, whose borders are just a few miles away, and they usually hang around here for the summer before heading back home. Animals do not recognise boundaries.

A little further away are fresh pugmarks. Two distinct sets actually. Tara has long gone but her wild progeny still abound around Billy's home, I fancy this place continues to be the tiger's haven. The tracker warns of the tiger's proximity. He's close, perfectly camouflaged in the tall grasses that surround me. I feel it again, that immense pleasure, with a shade of fear, the thrill of walking the tigers walk. Trailing his pugmarks, worrying, hoping that any moment this awesome predator will emerge. Silently behind me, or loom up ahead, blocking my path. The tense wait ends in an anti-climax. It is a no-show.

Later, after a scrumptious lunch, Billy takes a trip down memory lane, my appetite for tales of Tara and other felines is yet unsatiated. Tara loved aquatic sports, and was uncomfortably, never dangerously, fierce with her hugs. I find it hard to swallow that she, a tigress, would try to run up a tree when confronted with her canine pal, Elie.

But the realities of the present shadow the glories of the past. It is the bleak future of her kind that worries Billy. 'No one cares for the tiger, it has no future,' is now his despondent voice. In the three days that I stay, Billy impresses on me the urgency to save India's wildlife. To save ourselves. His constant refrain is, 'The air we breathe and the water we drink stem from the biodiversity of the universal environment. The tiger is at the centre of this truth. If it goes, we go.'

I ask Billy his one desire in life, certain he wished for a magic wand that would rejuvenate the dying tiger. Instead, he alights from his seat, walking steadily towards his weather-beaten music system, inserts the tape inside the deck and hands me the cover, gaudily decorated with pink hearts. I look at him in puzzlement, till the speakers cackle out a sound foreign in a drawing room but from the heart of the jungle. *Hon-HON, hon-HON*, accompanied by a lilting drone in the background, the Swamp Deer bugle resounds within the confines of the room. Billy has a hand in the survival of the *barasinghas* in Dudhwa, pushing them into the forest with the help of shikar elephants from fields where they fell prey to hunters. He looks

at me, now, his eyes beseeching, 'Can you please make me a horn with this sound? Do you know that the *barasingha* is Uttar Pradesh's state animal? Isn't it befitting then, that my jeep horn should echo with its rutting call?' I picture Billy, bumping along country roads, scaring the daylights of unsuspecting commuters with the jeep's rutting call. Yes, Billy, I answer, smiling through my tears.

When I came here, I was in awe of Billy, his books had instilled in me the urgency to conserve wildlife. Now, I am devoted to the man, so overwhelming is his devotion to the cause. He taught me another important lesson, something that has stood me in good stead in all my jungle wanderings. 'Never fear wild animals. They recognise your fear, and react. Be calm. Be confident. Animals know. They know that you mean them no harm. That you are their friend. They won't harm you.' Cynics will laugh and science will deride, but his words are embedded in my heart. They are a foundation for my faith.

The electricity is erratic but its absence is not felt. A thousand stars light the night and the cool breeze from the river beats the most powerful air-conditioner. Later, much later I can hear the faint call of a tiger, *Aaummm*. Delighted, I look across to Billy, his eyes sparkle, his face lights up, energised by the call of the beloved. The tiger is in its haven.

Yours

Prerna Singh Bindra

Meeting the Ancestors

Namdapha in Arunachal Pradesh has the proud distinction of being the only tiger reserve in India with four of India's five big cats: Tiger, Snow Leopard, Clouded Leopard and Leopard. All so elusive and so rare that their presence itself is an open question here. The rainforest shields them from the intrusive human eye. The felines are not much missed either, not in this riotous, unfathomable, immense rainforest. So overpowering that it sucks you into its primitive womb, entraps you in its gossamer web, enchants you with its bewitching beauty. No tigers here, but a memorable meeting with the Hoolock Gibbon, India's only ape and our close cousin in the wild, leaves me touched.

Delight is too weak a term to express the feelings of a naturalist who for the first time has wandered by himself in a rainforest.
Charles Darwin

As a child, my class was given an exercise: Paint the earth as it looked when God created it. I remember painting a riot of green, incredibly tall trees populated by monkeys and vivid birds, and, in the thick green carpet below, I drew childlike faces of the tiger. A blue river gushed through and colourful butterflies dotted this Garden of Eden. As I grew up this vision blurred; I had scoured much of India's wilderness, but nowhere did I find the unsullied forest of my juvenile imagination. Adult cynicism rationalised that in our ravaged planet, God's paradise had no place. Namdapha proved me wrong.

To echo Darwin, delight is too weak a term to describe my feelings as the jeep drove into the Namdapha Tiger Reserve. I go further than Darwin's description: I was enchanted, excited, thrilled, happy, elated, captivated, smitten but even that is insufficient to express my reaction to the rainforests of Namdapha.

The KING and I

Hoolock Gibbon

Like every other forest, it has trees. But they are unlike any other trees I have seen. Thousands of them, massive, immense and incredibly high. So tall that they look as if they would have dwarfed the twin towers that were brought down on 9/11. So tall that my neck ached from my attempts to view life on the canopy. They stand ramrod straight, spreading their branches wide. Each tree is akin to a tiny village with a bustling community life. Woodpeckers can be heard crafting their homes in branches, Malayan Squirrels gorge on fruits and Capped Langurs lounge on a cluster of trees. They are different from the drab black and white variety common back home; coat tinged with red, thighs painted a cobalt blue and they sport a jaunty cap. The langurs are a busy, noisy lot, crashing from one platform onto another, pausing for an occasional chat with each other. A lone Assamese Macaque wanders up and is chased away by the langurs. Later, in the night I spot the giant squirrel glide from one branch to another.

The trees have been named wisely. *Haathi payla* means elephant ear to represent the shape of the leaves while another tree is the *bandardima* owing to the fact that the monkey is partial to its red pomegranate-like fruit. The Strangler Fig is a selfish tree, 'just like man,'

Before rice-beer was invented life was very dull. Men sat around feeling bored; they had nothing to talk about; they did not hold council, tell stories or laugh...
Old tribal belief

quips the cook, for its branches stifle the host tree in a vice-like grip slowly killing it as it sucks out its nutrients.

The trees interlock, their thick vine-like branches in a cloying embrace create a contiguous wall of green. Giant trees wear garlands of orchids. The ground is wet and marshy – a tangled mass of wild grass, dead leaves, barks and bushes. The forest is a thousand shades of green, changing colours with the time of day and season. At dawn, the jungle is clear and bright, as the day progresses, the sun gets aggressive, piercing through the trees, its rays reflecting and glistening on the leaves and branches, as if a million lamps have been lit haphazardly in the forest.

Deban has to be one of the most beautiful places in the world, though architecturally speaking the forest resthouse could do better. It stands amidst the virginal (well, not really), rainforest with the Noedehing river flowing below. Noedehing has the clearest, bluest water I have ever seen and the first thing I do is scamper down to the bank to swallow a mouthful. It is a long trek but well worth the trouble. This stretch of rainforest is unique in the sense that it is perhaps the only forest in India which has, as I have pointed out earlier, four of India's

big cats; Snow Leopard, Tiger, Clouded Leopard and the Leopard. But big cat sightings are almost mythical and tiger tales are regaled and embellished from the pages of history. For instance, the story of the lucky girl who met a tigress with a cub six years ago, when trekking through the jungle. Then there was the ghost tiger. Phantom-like, always around, but never seen, just leaving its pugmarks, as big as an elephant's

– or so I am informed, with much relish. Another guard is utterly convinced he saw a leopard, olive green, army style! I take all this in with a pinch of salt. Under the influence of *apong*, the local brew, colours often change, proportions vary and memory plays games.

If you are a cat maniac, intent on sighting the tiger and his ilk, a visit here is 'useless'. In fact, sighting any animal, forget the big mammals, is a task impossible because the undergrowth is so dense. It is almost as though the forest had ganged up to provide cover to its denizens from man's prying eyes and evil intentions.

The rainforest has many secrets. In our arrogance we assume we know better, but ever so often, it springs pleasant surprises, introducing new residents or bringing back those believed to be lost and forgotten.

Namdapha should be packaged with a warning: 'Beware! This forest may change you for ever'. Namdapha possessed me, made me do strange things, like getting up at four in the morning, something I have rarely done. It got me thinking on the wisdom of living in the wear and tear of urban chaos. And now that I am back, its beauty still haunts me.

Not all is hunky dory, though. It's 6.20 am and I have spent the last two hours walking – or trying to – through narrow jungle paths, the way blocked repeatedly by vines and protruding branches, sometimes laden with sharp thorns and abrasive leaves. I lose my balance on the mushy floor and am soaked in slush.

And I am lost, in the blink of an eye; my guide, the efficient Mr Das, seems to have vanished in the vast thickness. I am reeling under the double attack of big red ants and slimy leeches. The ants have a vicious sting and the leeches cling tenaciously to my bare feet, and other exposed parts of the body. Feeding on my blood, these thin spindles swell into plum balloons. My legs, swathed in blood, look straight out of a horror film, though later I display the swollen welts like prized war medals!

At this moment, I am miserable. It is here, now, when I am lost among giants, that the enormity of the rainforest strikes me. I am insignificant, powerless in the unknown. Not a friend, not a known soul. There were tigers around and leopards, not to mention wild dogs

Deban Forest Resthouse

The KING and I

and wayward tuskers and I felt a lone tear slide down my cheek. *Hooooo looooo, Hooooolooooo.......* suddenly the forest resounds with loud whooping cries. I look up to see the Hoolock Gibbon, India's only ape and man's closest relative in the wild. The Hoolocks and I share ninety-eight per cent DNA. Scientific and local lore assert that they are our ancestors. They are marvellously agile, using their long arms to swing from one tree to another, jumping and gliding gracefully in search of succulent fruits and leaves. Did we, *Homo sapiens*, ever manage such incredible acrobatic feats? Somehow I doubt it.

My sense of desolation dims, my fear of being alone has turned into sheer delight in my encounter with our relatives. The male gibbon is jet black with his face slashed with thick white eyebrows, giving him a villainous look. He usually has one mate, but occasionally may expand his harem to three or four. *Bandar ke gale mein moti ki mala*. (The monkey wears a garland of jewels!) How true, I muse, as I gaze at the mismatched couple.

The female is a seductive, blond beauty. She sports a lush golden coat and climbs further down, gazing at me curiously. *Hooolooo, Hooolooo*, I imitate her call, and she ventures closer, tilting her head to give me a curious look. She answers back, a little uncertain, and soon we are chattering away as women are wont to, though she keeps a cautious distance. I am thrilled and touched. I have a strange feeling of bonding with my ancestors, crossing the species and generation barrier. This magical, almost unreal moment is broken by the arrival

of a very worried Mr Das. The gibbon scampers away. If I do not see anything, do nothing else in this forest, I do not care. The meeting with Mr and Mrs Gibbon is a memory that will stay with me forever.

Later in the night I experiment with *Kham*, the local rice beer, with the forest staff. They are mostly tribals and they tell me of the threat of the Lishu tribe which is known to hunt in the forests. It is a tradition that is hard to break, and everything from monkeys to elephants is food. Ke Kanglom is a forester and belongs to the Tutsa tribe. They hunt the wilds for the pot too, but spare the Hoolock. 'How,' asks Kanglom, 'can we kill our forefathers?' The same logic protects the Slow Loris – a primate so called because of its lethargic gait and measured movements. The loris, goes the local belief, is the 'retard' child of the monkey, had it been born right and without this 'genetic birth defect' it would have been the gibbon. I dare not question the scientific rationale; I am just glad that its demented tag has saved the loris from a brutal and gory end.

The Lishus and other tribes are traditional hunters. On my way to the forest I had halted at Changlang, where a congregation of tribals was celebrating *Mol*, the annual festival heralding a good harvest. The tribals were dressed in their traditional gear, a fascinating ensemble. The *khopu*, or their crown, was especially impressive though ecologically suicidal. The finely woven bamboo caps were ornamented with tusks of wild boar, coarse black bear hair and feathers of the endangered Great Hornbill. Some were crafted from leopard skin. Further on the Burma border at Khonsa, I met another tribe which in olden days did not restrict their hunt to the animal kingdom. The king of the Nocte tribe guided me to a room, a shelf on the wall was lined with human skulls, brittle and yellow with age. These were harvests of battles over land and honour. The spoils of the victory, or the skulls were usually brought back from the battlefield as testaments of victory. Once they were proudly displayed as symbols of power and courage, now, says the Pi Raja, they are an embarrassment and must be hidden from the law.

I deviate, but the crux of the matter is that hunting is a way of life in these parts, and I came across assorted hunting parties, hound in tow, who targeted anything that flew and moved. Earlier, such slaughter was

The KING and I

Rufous-necked Hornbill

limited for consumption and decoration purposes, but now traders lure tribals into commercial poaching. The impact on the forest is catastrophic, coupled with the illegal logging that continues even in the face of a Supreme Court ban. I despair, each Eden has its serpent, but before the poison swallows the forest, it must be protected. I ponder on the subject before I drift into deep sleep, occasionally punctuated by mysterious, wild calls.

Post ape, everything is an anti-climax. Though there is much to be said about the sheer pleasure of crossing blue waters in a wooden boat to land in a rich rainforest. The leeches are thrilled to see me again and latch on to my legs fiercely. By now, I am seasoned and dispose them off with a flourish. I can hear the gibbons above, though I do not see one. A barking deer flashes past. I desire to see the Rufous-necked Hornbill and other hornbill species Namdapha is famous for. Huge birds with massive 'double' beaks, the hornbill's nesting behaviour would raise the ire of a feminist. The incubating female is locked inside her nest in the hollow of a

Clouded Leopard

Next Page: Malayan Giant Squirrel

tree branch with the male carefully sealing off the opening. He leaves a tiny slit, just enough for him to pass food to his growing family.

Back at Deban, lunch is an exotic meal; we have picked up some wild fern and whipped up a delicious *sabzi* with the help of the cook. There is wild banana and *lichu*, the *litchi's* luscious wild cousin, which I suck happily. A wayward elephant interrupts the meal. The young tusker has wandered into the manicured lawns of the guesthouse and is systematically eating the carefully laid out plants. Pandemonium breaks out as cook, sidekick, *mali*, *chowkidar* shout and mutter obscenities to a supremely indifferent elephant. They return defeated and the animal exits later, leaving behind sufficient proof of its destructive prowess.

It was a domestic elephant, earlier used to extract timber, now banned by an order of the Supreme Court. A fallout has been that it has left behind an army of unemployed elephants, who earlier used to uproot timber. They have been left to their own devices by unscrupulous timber traders and such damaging interruptions are routine at Deban.

Leaving Namdapha is near impossible, I feel at home here and utterly content, in spite of being cut off from the civilised world and its myriad comforts. Why must I go? Work and looming deadlines are not sufficient motivation to leave this wild paradise and it is only the determination to come back for a longer spell that I can make the final wrench.

Death in Water

Sundarbans Tiger Reserve in West Bengal is the world's largest delta, this massive mangrove forest covers an area of 2585 square kilometres, with the highest number of tigers. 270 at last count, a number open to question. Sundarbans, however, cannot be dismissed with such banalities. It is an inexplicable region, where land merges into water. It is tide country, where life is governed by the rise and fall of the tide. The tigers live by different rules, too. Man is part of their diet, though conversely it is this macabre trait that has saved the fragile ecology of Sundarbans. Here also lives Bonobibi, the secular Goddess of Hindus and Muslims alike, protecting man from tiger. Not always though, for here, death lurks in the water.

I wonder if God was playing a game when he created Sundarbans: for nowhere else is beauty so arduous, so volatile, as though exacting a price for its presence. Those who live here must pay a cost, either with their life or by their sweat and blood.

No rules bind Sundarbans, either man or nature's. It has a law of its own, parallel to none on earth. A vast archipelago of islands, fifty-two at last count, some ancient, others of a recent origin; some gigantic, others so small you could walk their length in minutes. The geography is constantly shifting; land becomes water and water, land. It is a region without borders, lacking divisions between the river and the sea, between fresh and salt water. Even land and water seem indistinguishable as one merges into the other along blurred lines. It's as though God wanted to retain control over some fraction of the earth, preserve a mystery that man is unable to fathom.

The KING and I

Bonobibi shrine at Sajnekhali

Sundarbans is a forest bizarre where myriad eco-systems – land, marine, riverine, mangrove – co-exist, separately and collectively. It hosts uncanny denizens: Fish 'walk' on land, roots reach for the sky instead of digging deep into the earth, animals drink salt water, and the tigers…ah, the tigers, unlike any on earth. So deviant is their behaviour than their kin elsewhere, that there exists a whispered belief that they are a separate species altogether. Wherever they reign, tigers are more than mere animals. Here, in this delta, tigers are stuff legends and myths are made of. It swims, it flies and it eats man. It is invisible, it is omnipotent. It is God, it is Demon, it is revered, it is hated. It protects the forest; it feasts of the flesh of man. The tiger is all-powerful, it appears from nowhere and gets bigger by the minute. It launches itself from water, it flies though the air. It lands weightlessly on boats, carries human prey unseen, unheard and vanishes in the swirling waters.

The tiger of the Sundarbans is a mystery. How does it survive on salt water and swim in the sea? And more importantly, why does it relish man? As a rule, tigers are rarely man-eaters. It is believed that they are driven to hunt man when weakened by age or injury to kill their natural prey. The Sundarbans tiger, however, has man on its menu. J Fayrer, who coined the term Royal Bengal Tiger, estimated in 1886 that in a period of six years the tiger devoured 4,218 people. The carnage continued, though in recent years the killings have abated and in 2003, the tiger claimed just eight lives.

No one has answers to this alarming propensity for human meat, but various theories, from the ridiculous to the plausible, have been floated. Some attribute its tastes to the tidal ecology, citing that the constant shift of land and water makes the tiger disoriented and aggressive; while others say that its ferocity is linked to its diet of salt water. Perhaps the marshy, oozy terrain makes hunting difficult and man, an easier prey. The solutions to the menace have been equally fantastic, digging sweet water holes, putting face masks on the back of the head since it is believed that tigers never attack head-on. Another bright idea was to fool the tiger by scattering life-size dummies suffused with human scent in strategic islands. These were mannequin woodcutters squatting on the ground and dummy honey collectors, engineered to give an electric shock when disturbed. But the Sundarbans tiger is no fool, it simply tore the dummy to pieces and walked away.

Nothing has really worked. The death toll may have ebbed, though it is argued that majority of the deaths go unreported, but the fear hasn't.

The people's only shield against the wrath of the tiger is Bonobibi, the Goddess of the Forest. It is in her that they put their faith. No one, be it fisherman, honey collector, poacher or forest guard ventures out without invoking Ma Bonobibi. She rules the jungle; tigers, crocodiles and other animals do her bidding. And in a land plagued by communal strife, she is a uniting factor. Both Hindus and Muslims are her fervent devotees; after all, tigers are neither partial to, nor prejudiced against, any faith. They hunt without discrimination.

Which is why, perhaps, her legend is born not in Hindustan, but in Arabia. The story begins when the pregnant Gulalbibi is discarded by her husband, Ibrahim, urged on by his first wife, Fulbibi. Abandoned in the forest, fairies assisted her as she gave birth to twins. Finding the jungle hostile, a frightened Fulbibi fled with her son, leaving the tiny girl behind. Nurtured at the breast of a cheetal, and protected by Allah, Bonobibi grew up to be the Goddess of the Forest. When her twin, Shah Jungli, came to take her back, she knew that she must live in the Sundarbans, where she was destined to protect the people.

Myth has it that for centuries, Dakshin Ray, the tiger God, ruled the jungle with his army of crocodiles, ghosts and other malevolent spirits. And he lusted for human flesh. One day, he heard the strange sounds of the *azan*, the call to prayer in the jungle: Bonobibi and Shah Jungli had intruded his realm. He turned his wrath on them, unleashing his army of ghouls and demons. But Bonobibi won unarmed, and, merciful in her victory, she divided the spoils. The wilds would henceforth be Dakshin Ray's domains, the

Bonobibi and Shah Jungli

Human dummy

The KING and I

Tiger hunt. Nineteenth century

rest she claimed would belong to the people. And so the balance remained for a long time, till man's greed intruded into the tiger's empire.

The story shifts to more recent times. Dukhey, meaning sad, was a poor, orphaned boy who was duped by the evil merchant Donna to be a sacrifice to Dakshin Ray in lieu of honey and other gifts of the forest. Terrified, Dukhey called for Bonobibi to come and rescue him and she dispatched Shah Jungli to defeat Dakshin Ray. Dukhey was later adopted by Bonobibi, who built him a splendid palace and found him a beautiful wife. In reality, Bonobibi is not just the Goddess of the forest; she reigns over all of Sundarbans. So deeply is she imbibed in the psyche of the people that she is no longer a myth. She is the biggest truth in the tide country.

White-bellied Sea Eagle

Mudskippers

About four million people live in this hostile terrain, and while they know the risks involved, they must intrude into Dakshin Ray's domain for fish, honey and wood. For sheer survival they face death, every day. There are other Gods that the locals seek: Goddess Mansa is worshipped to satisfy venomous snakes; Jagatpuri is a special God appointed to handle the deadly cobra; Olaichandi fights cholera while Satyanarayan-Satya Pir is for general welfare.

Man likes to imagine himself at the apex of the ecological pyramid, a supreme being in perfect control of his environment. His pompous assumption is not off the mark for his ingenuity has overcome what God denied him. He has changed the course of rivers, reduced dense forests to wastelands and tamed ferocious beasts. In Sundarbans, nature has fought back. This riverine delta has a mind of its own, changing course and swamping land at will; the tide governs man and animal: they must obey the rhythm of *jowar* and *bhatta*, the flood and ebb. And man is at the mercy of tiger and crocodile.

That such a mystic land exists at all, in the present age, is a revelation. That it is within calling distance from the teeming metropolis of Kolkata is more astounding. It takes me a little over two hours to drive to Sonakhali, past noisy bazaars, paddy fields and individual ponds dug outside thatched huts in a vain attempt to satisfy the east Indian yearning for fish. The *ghat* at Sonakhali is nothing more, nothing less than a boisterously noisy quintessential Indian railway station, except that the mode of transport here is water-borne. Most of the crowd is gathered here for their routine 'up-down' journey between islands and the mainland for work and daily necessities. Others are a raucous band of the most enthusiastic travellers in India, the Bengalis, in nervous anticipation of seeing the 'bagh.'

I escape the madding crowds to get on the ultimate luxury these waters offer, *Pugmark*, a motorised launch all to myself, with a sun-deck to perch on, a bed to sleep in, a kitchen to

The KING and I

provide meals and, the best of all, a clean bathroom. It might seem inconsequential to the urbanite but when the only option is to step onto land and risk being a tiger's meal, the toilet gains supreme importance. Even the most basic dingy here fashions one of sorts since it brings bad luck to soil the tiger's domain. Nothing of the man must remain in the territory earmarked for Dakshin Ray, claims local lore.

Initially, the reality of Sundarbans does not sink in, bustling villages rest on its banks and overloaded arks pass by. But as the boat glides sensuously over the water, villages get scantier, the mangroves denser and land a mere whisper. There is just you, the water and the sky. And the hundred myths that the forest lives by.

You are lucky, says Babu, our boatman. Not even halfway to our destination, and a ripple in the placid water reveals a fin, then a rounded snout. From his aquatic home an *Orcealla brevirostris*, the Irrawady dolphin, emerges to take in a breathe of fresh air. Virtually unheard of till recently, this dolphin entered the limelight and people's conscious, as protagonist of Amitav Ghosh's award-winning novel, *The Hungry Tide*. It is a rare creature, surviving in such small numbers that their future is questionable. Seeing one is even rarer. But that is not why Babu deems me fortunate. Folklore does not confine this mammal as a mere dolphin, it is blessed as the messenger of Bonobibi. In high tide they roam the forests, becoming her eyes and ears; when the tide ebbs they tell her the secrets they have learnt. It is a good omen. Babu smiles; it meant that Bonobibi would know we had entered her dominion. She would protect us from all evil. She would protect us from the tiger.

I do not echo Babu's delight. A city girl, I have little faith in the forest Goddess. Besides, I would rather not be denied the tiger. I would prefer to be that rare person who saw the

Sundarbans tiger. But that was before I met those lucky enough to escape the jaws of death. The tiger had left its deadly imprint in each village, each home had a horror story to tell. Babu points out Goshaba, infamous as the tiger widow village. I shivered, the tiger is a gentleman, isn't he? Then why does the tiger predate humans? Why does man become meat?

For now, man-eaters seem another person's nightmare. Rocking gently in the breast of the sea, the *Pugmark* carries me to my destination, the island of Bali. Not as glamorous as its namesake in Indonesia, but certainly as beautiful in its rusticity. My home here is the Bali Island Resort. I am prepared to make this my permanent abode. It has been set up by an enterprising group of youngsters, who were once ultra left extremists or the Naxalites, now doing their bit for conservation of the forests and boosting the local economy.

Such lofty motives do not concern me, occupied as I am with the delicious local fare and stories narrated by a gang of ex-poachers. Anil was treed by the tiger the very first day he ventured in, to shoot spotted deer for the pot. He clung to the tree, the predator waited patiently below for his meal. Providence — no, Bonobibi, he corrects — rescued him. Another tells of his equally daring escape, this time from the forest department.

Morning dawns, beginning with a visit to the resident Bonobibi shrine. The temple, housed in a hut, is dominated by her brightly painted idol bedecked in a vivid red sari and the equally elaborately dressed Shah Jungli. Dakshin Ray, poor

The KING and I

chap, is a little clay figure wearing stripes of black and gold, lurking amongst the giants. The villagers have made a statement: May the powers of Bonobibi overpower that of the tiger. I resume my aquatic journey. I do not know it yet, but later I will mark the date as a red-letter day on my calendar, as the occasion I missed a glimpse of the infamous man-eating tiger of Sundarbans. By a minute, or so. Everyone thought I was incredibly lucky. I thought otherwise.

Till this opportune moment, the jungle divulges its other wonders. Trees stand in the water on stilts and a Mangrove Whistler, a very rare but nondescript bird, flutters in the twine and tangle of the roots. A White-bellied Sea Eagle swoops on the water and emerges seconds later with a fish gripped in its talons. Tiny fish with tinier 'legs' in front walk on the ooze, which I learn are mudskippers. Anil points out the Hental Tree with thorns so big that once they pierce your skin the only way you can extract them is to insert the hollow end of a key. My luck with dolphins continues: a Bottle-nosed dolphin virtually unseen in this delta rips through the water. It is a drab creature, painted in dull grey, but is a friendly sort, known to swim close to boats and help fishermen drive shoals of fish into their nets.

The next sighting is not as friendly. The creature most feared in these parts after the tiger, and with almost as many murders to its credit, is the crocodile. The *kumir*, as it is locally called, is sunning itself on the bank, at one with the mud, waiting for an unsuspecting victim.

The boat has wedged itself into a narrow creek in the park's core area, courtesy a special permit from the forest department. The mood changes, intangibly. I can feel the tension in the air; the guide shifts uncomfortably, his back stiff, as though readying for a hasty departure. Babu darts nervous glances as he skillfully manoeuvres the boat. Two people are stationed at both ends to keep a sharp eye for uninvited feline guests. Nothing is left to

Estuarine Crocodile

chance. The marshy banks hem us in; the tiger could appear at any moment, launch itself on the boat, carry back its meal – one of us. Too quick even for the rest of us to realise.

'Those who see *mama* here do not live to tell the tale,' warns Babu quietly. *Mama*? Here in this forest you never utter or even think the word tiger or *bagh*. It is taboo. It is disrespectful. It is inviting danger. Hence the locals call it *mama*, the Hindi equivalent for maternal uncle. I notice huge imprints the size of a giant human hand on the wet sand. The mark of the tiger. He had just been here, for the tide had ebbed only ten minutes ago; the tiger had come thereafter. I am sure he is here somewhere, my hands shake as I hastily, nervously take pictures. I do not need to see the tiger: I can sense it, hidden somewhere in the dense jungle beyond, watching each move we made. We leave, and I realise that tigers are the great invisibles here, rarely seen but omnipresent, prowling the fringes of our imagination, dominating each mood and every step we take in their domain.

In Bali, that night, my hosts decide to honour Bonobibi, as a grateful gesture for keeping a protective eye on us. A *jatra* or a folk play, *The Glory of Bonobibi* is to be performed by local artists. Preparations have begun in earnest, and as is wont on such occasions, confusion reigns supreme. The crisis is that Bonobibi, or rather the star who is to play her, is not to be found. All sorts of explanations for her non-appearance are dished out: She has run off with the boatman; she had too much *hadia* — the local brew — and passed out; her mother-in-law has locked her in. The crisis is resolved by a replacement, a rather insipid character, though she made up with sheer enthusiasm.

The *jatra* is well orchestrated, and the performance of Dukhey, by a tragic looking young girl, would have put a professional to shame. The costumes are garish, and nothing about the baggy striped outfit or the clay mask Dakshin Ray wore invoked terror. But when he springs

The KING and I

The Glory of Bonobibi being enacted

inside with a terrifying roar, the fear in Dukhey's face is mirrored among all. 'Ma Bonobibi, amake bachao,' cries Dukhey, and in sweeps the Goddess, a trifle late, having paused out to spew the *paan* she was chewing. She saves Dukhey, gifts him with riches, and a wife, and sends him home astride a crocodile! There isn't a dry eye in the audience, which incidentally comprises the entire village, assembled to applaud the unexpected entertainment.

Amidst the merry-making I note that the prompter is reading the script of the Bonobibi backwards. *The Glory of Bonobibi* is scripted in Urdu but the language is Bangla. Enacted and held sacred by both Hindus and Muslims. Here, I think, on this obscure island, secularism is ingrained in daily life. Nothing is pretentious. All seek Bonobibi, she belongs to no religion. It's a perfect thought to end a momentous day.

I wake up to clear skies. It is time to depart. It is a wrench; Sundarbans has a way of getting under your skin, embedding itself deep inside your being. But it is more than that. My stay has not answered any questions and Sundarbans remains as much a mystery as ever. The answers are impregnable, as entangled as the roots of the mangroves themselves.

Idris Ali helps, though. He is an oddity here, attacked by a tiger and lived to tell the tale. He is a honey collector. Every year the forest department issues permits to harvest the hives and though these were earmarked for specific areas, Idris' boat ventured deeper into forbidden territory. It was riskier, but the hives were heavier and aplenty. It was a good day too, the first day of Baisakh, the harvest festival, and nothing could go wrong. It did. Among his cronies, Ali is considered fearless and hence, he is usually the one entrusted with the most dangerous job, to survey the forest for potential man-eaters before the rest of the team disembarks. He had a spear with him for defense. 'If you think the Bonobibi will protect

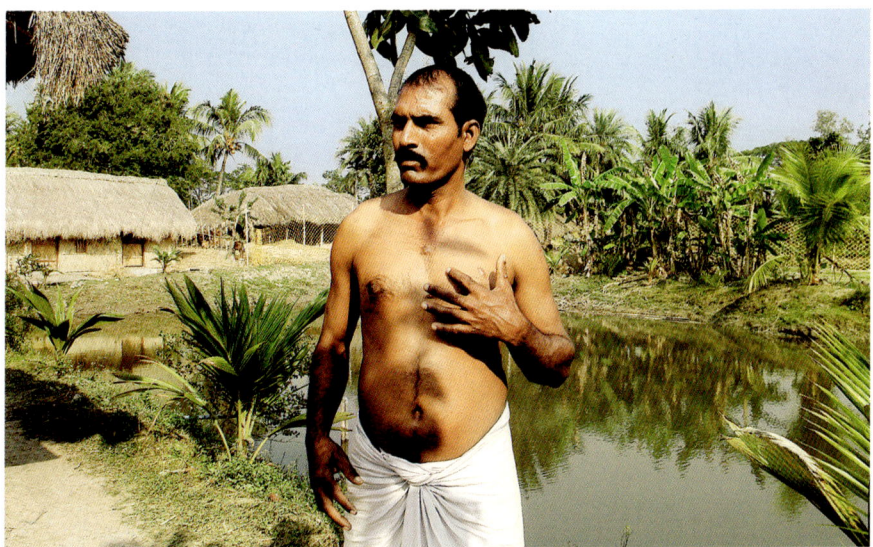

Idris Ali

while you lie comatose, then you are dead meat. She only helps those who help themselves,' affirms Ali.

The tiger jumped at him from behind a tiny tree, one that couldn't possibly shield a rat. One mighty paw imprisoned his head, another pressed against his chest with the vicious canines barely an inch away from his own. Ali fought back 'I have to stay upright,' he remembers thinking, 'else I will die.' He used his spear, the tiger roared. Long, painful seconds ticked by, the water underneath reddened with blood. His and the tiger's. A long struggle ensued, but he was saved. How, he doesn't know. Was it his presence of mind or his nephew who hit the tiger on the head with the paddle taking the animal by surprise? And certainly, the benevolence of Bonobibi.

Ali glances at the wounds, tugging his ravaged flesh. 'We are all tiger meat,' he whispers, 'Humans imagine themselves above all, but no, here we are just plain food.'

The encounter has bequeathed no scars on his mind. He is not scared to again enter Dakshin Ray's jungle. He has a family of seven and he must go to collect wood and honey. The forest feeds them. And the tiger? He protects the forest. Ali is a simple man, educated up till class four. But he taught me what all the years of education, fancy conferences and tomes on ecology couldn't. 'It is man who destroys the forest. If the tiger had not been there, we would have flattened the jungles, culled the mangroves, hunted the animals and ravaged the land. We would have starved and without the protection of the trees, the tide would have swallowed us all. The tiger kills but occasionally, it is only a warning. If we destroy his and our home, we will all perish.' That is the reality of Sundarbans; it is the man-eaters of this mighty delta who save the beautiful forest, the Sundarbans.

Kipling Country

Rudyard Kipling does not require an introduction. His most loved work, The Jungle Book, was based in the forests of Central India. Kanha and Pench Tiger Reserves in Madhya Pradesh claim their connection with Kipling. It is in these verdant grasslands and forests that the 'man cub' Mowgli was brought up by his assorted four-legged guardians — the endearing Baalu, the wily panther Kaa and the King of the Jungle, Sher Khan. Legendary man-cubs are relics of the past, but Sher Khan lives on in the tiger state of India. Kanha is a special forest, rich with predator and prey. It is also home to the endangered Swamp Deer or the barasingha. Pench transcends two states, Maharashtra and Madhya Pradesh and lies tucked under the Seoni hills.

A foray into Mowgli land, where Nobel laureate Rudyard Kipling based his classic *The Jungle Book* was a childhood fantasy come true. Kanha, famous for its tigers, has always attracted tourists while Pench, still a fledgling destination was eager to do so. Both were packaging themselves as Mowgli's land. It was an interesting assignment, to discover the forests through a classic fictional fantasy that was eerily real. *The Jungle Book* became my bible and I clung to it as I traced the path Mowgli and his assorted animal friends haunted, exploring the jungle where Bagheera the Panther, Kaa the Python and Baalu the affable bear took the man cub as their own and taught him jungle craft. I visited the village where Mowgli was born and ultimately destined to return — yes, even though the character is fictional, the locales are real. I would be lying, though, if I said I was following Kipling's footsteps, for truth to tell, the author, oddly enough, had never set foot in the Central Provinces of India, the region he brings to life in his book.

The KING and I

Wild Dogs

The journey begins at the Pench Tiger Reserve. Mowgli's jungles are encircled by the Seonee (now called Seoni) Hills in Central India, where the wolf pack lived and hunted and brought up the man-cub. The reserve lies partially in Maharashtra, while the larger part is housed in India's tiger state, Madhya Pradesh. Pench stretches to more than 600 square kilometres of dry deciduous forests and houses an impressive list of rare fauna, that include the tiger, leopard, gaur, dhole, Bonelli's Eagle, Painted Spur Fowl to name but a few.

The first rule when you travel in the forests is to 'be prepared' for the unexpected. Nature does not adhere to rules, she is temperamental and carries you along her whimsical moods. The lesson I imbibe is to revel in each facet, rather than grumble about the discomfort the sudden changes might bring. It's bright and sunny when I enter Pench, the kind of day you would devote to a picnic. Within minutes, however, the heavens open and water pours through. Not a drizzle, but a proper downpour. The thunder bellows in anger, the wind tears at the trees and lashes at our vehicle. Darkness descends rapidly. And the sharp, silver flash of lightning illuminates the forest in blinding flashes. The sudden onslaught washes away the *kutcha* roads. We have to stop periodically to remove branches that block our path. A *nullah* proves difficult to manoeuvre and we wind a tedious, bumpy path only to halt within a few meters of the Karmajhiri forest guesthouse.

The small check dam constructed by the forest department to help the animals through the summer has given way and water envelopes the road. I can see no trace of land, just a mass of raging water.

There is no way that the jeep can wade through. The effort to clear blocked paths has failed, though I have become thoroughly drenched in the process. I am shivering with cold and racked with hunger. Just across the swollen stream, so near yet out of reach, is the resthouse, softly illuminated by candles. I look toward the sky and prepare myself for a long wait, if the rain gods have come to stay.

It's not easy, the darkness and the quirky flashes of lightning conjure unwanted images. The friendly Bagheera of *The Jungle Book* morphs into a hungry panther, Sher Khan could be lurking somewhere close, disguised by the night. Jay Kumar, the driver, does not help either. He thinks it wise to keep me amused by telling me tall tales of a certain unfriendly leopard who had once frequented these paths. Just as I am about to give myself up to despair, the radio in the jeep comes to life, conveying the message that the park director, worried about us stranded, is on his way. Some time later, he arrives, assures me that all is fine, ushers me in his jeep and turns the vehicle back.

He thinks it wise to make good use of our time, he had spotted a herd of gaur and the promise of this unexpected pleasure makes me forget my discomfort and fear.

Initially, I can sight nothing, what spreads before me is a sea of darkness. The jeep's dimmed headlights are switched on and slowly bring to light numerous pin-point eyes, looking not unlike pairs of tiny torches suspended mid air. Gradually, my eyes attune to the darkness and I detect bulky forms. Then the sky throws in light, for a mere second, allowing us an amazing spectacle of dozens of gaurs, huge males weighing nearly a ton, watchful mothers with frisky young calves, looking oddly comical in their bedraggled, wet gear.

Back to the overflowing *nullah*, we decide to abandon the jeep and take our chances wading though the torrent of water. It is a slippery path, we stumble through, interrupted by

The KING and I

Gaur

a snake, swirling along with the tide. Kumar plucks it by the tail, tosses it aside, and both the snake, and us, make our way to safety.

We finally reach the warmth of the resthouse, where piping hot coffee and warm food await us. The resthouse is extremely comfortable and picture-book pretty, but tough luck if you are addicted to your cell phone and daily dose of TV soaps. In a sense, staying here is akin to travelling back in time: no newspapers, silence interrupted not by the telephone ring but the insistent *krrrriiich* of beetles and myriad other forms of life. There is a television, but only for appearance's sake. In my three separate visits, it has never worked. Thank God!

I leave for our jungle run at dawn. Perhaps I shall see Sher Khan? The cacophony of alarm calls indicates that the tiger is around. Our elephant extends her trunk forward, sniffing the air, heavy with the pungent odour of tiger. That's all the tiger I get that day. We move on, past landscapes dotted by cheetals and to our big sighting of the day, a pair of wolves, promptly lost in the undergrowth. Wolves, in India and elsewhere, are tagged with a notoriety they rarely deserve, maligned as child-lifters, condemned as the big bad wolf. But in my Jungle Book, the canids I meet are the wise wolf pack of Seoni that helped nurture young Mowgli.

Pench/Kanha

In Pench, I am confronted by our paradoxical stance towards the tiger. Awe for its power and beauty. Feared as a carnivore. Killed for commerce. Venerated as God. I stop to pay homage at the Bagh Baba Mandir, a shrine for the 'Tiger God'. The small temple is awash with congealed blood, the Gonds, a local tribe had sacrificed a goat the previous night. I can see other offerings — corncobs, assorted harvest like a shaft of wheat and a grotesque necklace of chicken legs. Local lore demands that the devotees offer their 'harvest' to the tiger, a farmer may leave wheat, those with livestock will sacrifice an animal. The tiger must be appeased, he is a symbol of fertility. If he is happy, they will be blessed with a child, and the fields will flourish. The Gonds respect nature and traditionally their tombstones are brightly painted with animals, birds and trees. I am instructed to leave a tribute, and as words are my livelihood I leave at the feet of the tiger, a humble pen!

At night, our meal is interrupted by a commotion outside. A cobra has appeared in the premises. It hisses and slithers, but in minutes is efficiently packed in a jute bag by the foresters. I get into the jeep and we ceremoniously release the snake deeper in the jungle. We watch it glide deep into the jungle and freedom. Who needs secondhand excitement from the idiot box, when you can personally star in an adventure series, I ponder as I fall into deep and dreamless slumber.

The next day is reserved for Kanhiwada, a two-hour drive from Pench. Time has taken its toll in what must have been a picturesque village. I am pleasantly surprised to find that true to the classic, Kanhiwada is a potter's village. Mowgli was born in a potter's family and

The KING and I

pottery continues to dominate the economy. But not a soul here is aware that Kipling borrowed their village and immortalised it in literature. The name Mowgli rings a bell, but no thanks to the author. *The Jungle Book* has been adapted in an animated Hindi TV serial and the ditty that opened the episode had penetrated through to this obscure town. *"Chaddi pahan ke phool khila hai, phool khila hai,"* chirps an elfin child, as she hears the buzz around the jungle boy. This literally translates into, a flower has blossomed wearing an underwear! It implies the joy that a new flower-like child brings into the jungle, and the bewilderment of the guardian-animals who find it different from their cubs. Interestingly, there was a real wolf child around these parts, though very unlike the impish, fictional Mowgli. The book, *A Journey into the Kingdom of Oude* (1849) by William Sleeman documents a wolf child caught by his deputy in Sonadungri in Seoni. This 'man cub' had reportedly killed thirty-one people and was around seventeen when he was caught.

We move on to Sidhbaba Ghat, a very deep gorge in the Wainganga river, and the possible inspiration of Kipling's 'gorge of marble rocks', where Sher Khan hunted. Mowgli called it the 'Place of Death', but the huge rocks that plunge into the deep waters of the Wainganga do not deter local boys, who jump nimbly from one immense rock to the other.

Kanha is my next, much-awaited destination. The drive from Pench to Kanha Tiger Reserve is a nerve-racking, backbreaking, dry stretch of 180 kilometres. Kanha too lays claim to being Kipling country, given the fact that it is nestled in the Central Provinces.

Frankly, I have ceased to care one way or the other about the Kipling connection, seduced by the overpowering beauty of the rich *sal* forests of Kanha. Congested traffic and exhaust fumes of the highway have been replaced by crisp, clear air and the refreshing green of paddy fields loses itself to the forest, their uniformity taken over by unruly wilderness. The landscape appears lifeless, stark. Then a sambhar nervously darts across the road cutting through the forest, langurs halt their chatter to peer intently, a rare leopard cat (wow!) quickly darts into the undergrowth. I am exhilarated by this profusion of animals even before I enter the precincts of the sanctuary, and there is more to follow. I am welcomed at Kisli, the forest resthouse, by a curious cheetal fawn, who hesitantly inches towards me. I stand still, waiting, but the magic is shattered by the blaring horn of an oncoming vehicle,

Potter at Kanhiwada

tourists uncaring about the rules of the jungle. The fawn scampers to safety and nuzzles its agitated and relieved mother.

I arrive in the evening, too late for a safari. I settle outside, attuned to the throb of the jungle. Sounds unaccustomed to the urban ear. A golden oriole is singing its lilting number, *chuk chuuk*, goes an owlet, the beetle drones on, a decided irritant. Past midnight, I still refuse to leave my vigil on the verandah. A thousand stars light up the sky, carelessly patterned as though haphazardly strewn by the powers above. The eyes of a hundred cheetal, spread across the garden, glitter a few feet from me. My ears pick up a faint, grating, sawing sound. A leopard. The sound delivers an instant, momentous impact on the deer, who thunder away, as one in the stampede, a river of white spots fading into nothingness.

At the break of dawn, I join the waiting gaggle of noisy tourist cars, their excitable cacophony clashing with the peace of the forest. How, I wonder, is it possible to successfully marry tourism with wildlife?

I am lucky. Not even two minutes down the road, I spot the extremely rare Barasingha or swamp deer, a stag sporting its promised crown of a dozen antlers, magnificently silhouetted against the sky. It's unusual to see a lone deer, these are gregarious creatures, living in herds of various sizes and were once found extensively in central and north India. They were almost wiped out in Kanha as well, though the reserve now sports viable numbers.

A short nap after a hearty home-cooked meal and I am off for the afternoon round. I add gaur and the Changeable Hawk Eagle to the list of animals sighted, but there is no sign of the tiger. I try to convince myself that it doesn't matter, but deep in my heart I long to see the tiger. I couldn't quite leave without meeting Sher Khan, could I?

The KING and I

It's nearing dusk and we are on our way out when, suddenly, a tiger fills the path ahead. She is a tigress, and it occurs to me, foolishly, that she had responded to my fervent plea. She moves, no, glides towards us, so silent is her movement, so graceful her stealth. Her skin burns like tarnished gold in the fading sunlight. She is breathtakingly beautiful. She stops not ten feet from the vehicle, her eyes piercing mine, unblinking. I hold her stare, and wonder: She is so powerful, she can kill us with a single blow. She is so vulnerable, from people who persecute for her coat and bones. Why does she trust us, me, after what man has done to her kind? It is a moment frozen in time.

Swamp Deer

Then she puts one foot forward. Halts. The tigress tilts her head, curiously, as though contemplating her next move, judging whether we are trustworthy. She moves forward and walks unhurriedly past me, so close that her warm smell envelopes me. Had I moved my hand I could have touched her...

Elated, I sleep. Next day, we visit the tiger on elephant accompanied by some forest officials. It's a rather grand entourage, three of us saddled on separate elephants.

I climb Hemavati, a young, fine-looking park elephant. The mahout Sur Singh expertly guides Hemavati, stopping short of a rather large tiger. He is Bhura, a tiger past his prime, a Casanova, but unlike most tigers, a magnanimous one, who does not mind sharing his women with the younger lot. He is ardently pursuing a tigress, who doesn't share his passion. That is of no consequence to Bhura, he lunges for her and she snarls in anger. Before letting out a full-throated roar, a sound so potent it seems to split the sky. Hemavati lurches in fright and I am tossed backwards, one foot mercifully hooked in the folds of the *paikhana*, hovering inches above a snarling tigress and her extremely frustrated male. 'Bagh Baba,' I pray feverishly, 'spare me,' before Sur Singh pulls me back to safety.

In spite of the terrifying experience, I would have liked to linger on, such is the magnetic pull of the tiger, but a sense of shame for intruding into the tiger's privacy takes over, forcing

my departure. That night I read another tome, authored by Dunbar Brander, that I have acquired along the way. His descriptions speak of a verdant forest. He writes of his visit to Kanha in early nineteenth century. 'I have seen 1,500 head consisting of 11 different species in an evening stroll'. When he visited two decades later, the diminishing of fauna was visible, 'it is nothing like that now, but it contains more numbers and more species than any other tract of its size in Asia', he said. Kanha is still a wealthy forest, but game has thinned even further.

Kanha remains an important habitat today, crucial for the continual survival of the tiger in India, since it is large enough to host a viable population. Call it a natural wonder if you will, a garden of Eden that must be saved.

The Enchanted Forest

Manas is home to three big cats: Tiger, Leopard and the elusive Clouded Leopard. Besides, Manas has over twenty species of globally threatened animals. For some fauna, like the Hispid Hare and the Pygmy Hog, this forest is the only refuge. A blond simian, the Golden Langur, inhabits the canopy by the river Manas. And Manas offers an even rarer commodity — tranquillity. Strange, peace in a jungle ruled and ravaged by the gun for over two decades. But then, over the years, Manas has worked its magic even on the most hardened heart. Poachers with a macabre record are today diligently protecting the animals they once killed. They now work with the forest guards, their bitter enemy of yesteryears. That is the miracle of Manas. Little wonder then, that this forest holds a multitude of titles: World Heritage Site, Biodiversity Hotspot and a Tiger Reserve.

All that is said about Manas is an exaggeration, a hyperbole beyond the realm of possibility. 'It's heaven on earth,' promised a friend. An article dating back a decade said, 'if God ever thought of settling on earth, Manas would be his chosen home'. I take it all with a pinch of salt; these are old grandma stories. I figure nostalgia has tinged memory with a rosy hue, a yearning for paradise lost. Almost. For years the park was closed to visitors. Even when it partially threw its gates open, visitors stayed away. For over two decades, extremists held Manas under siege, and lawlessness reigned. Peace had given way to savagery, the silence broken not by the roar of the tiger or the trumpet of an elephant but by the crack of a gun. Animals were slaughtered indiscriminately, so were the people. Infrastructure was destroyed, trees were cut and grasslands flattened. Now, the tide has turned and the colour of death no longer bloodies the pristine blue of the river Manas.

The KING and I

Great Hornbills

I finally travel to this reserve in early 2005, intrigued by its history and its turning fortunes, skeptical of all the fairy tales I have accumulated about the wonders of this fabled land. I drive past golden grasslands so tall and dense they hide even the bulky silhouettes of elephant herds, their presence advertised only by the occasional squeal of their young. Then the woodlands begin, lush green foliage preceeding the tangle of trees, vines and creepers. Timid barking deer dash for cover, while the bolder sambhar look on curiously, almost disdainfully at our noisy contraption. Unlike the crowded tiger reserves of Ranthambhore and Bandhavgarh, where vehicles are virtually a part of the scenery, the denizens of Manas are yet unaccustomed to gawking humans. The road veers towards the aging, yet utterly charming Mothanguri forest resthouse, atop a hillock by the mighty Manas. Vividly coloured

Capped Langurs chatter incessantly on the branches above. Brilliant Fairy Bluebirds contrast with the bright red flower of silk cotton and the Golden Oriole regales us with his haunting melody. I spot a hare hopping urgently into the bushes and my heart misses a beat; I am certain it's the Hispid Hare, a greener, bulkier version of the common variety. It was thought to be extinct, till rediscovered in Manas. As it turns out, it is a case of mistaken identity, but the imagination flies free in the wild, and if I err, who cares?

    I close my eyes. The gurgling, gushing sound of the emerald blue river takes over my senses; the fresh, clear air soothes my jagged nerves. Nothing said on Manas is an embellishment, if anything even the greatest eulogy is an understatement. It is the refuge of the divine, a gift to us mortals.

The KING and I

Author on patrol

It is an unusual morning, a pleasant contrast from the polluted, grey dawn back home. I walk down the river – so clear that I catch my own reflection. The water murmurs, gurgles then crashes as it gathers speed over the rocks, unaware that it is an international border. Overhead, a storm breaks, it is the whooshing and honking of Great Hornbills as they fly across the river, from India into the Royal Kingdom of Bhutan. Even from this vertical distance I can recognise the bulk of this bird with its outlandish curved beak.

Crossing frontiers is a ritual, often repeated in the course of the day. I am told that Bhutan, with its concentration of fruiting trees, is the feeding ground of the hornbills and India is where they come home to roost. In the nesting season the male brings back the 'daily fruit', while his lady brings up the kids, locked by him in a hollow of a tree. He feeds her through a slit and it is a partnership that has stood the strength of time. Later in the day I witness a courting couple. They sit close together. Then the male forages in the tree, testing several figs for their ripeness. He selects one and runs the fruit to and fro in his beak, mashing it to a pulp. With unexpected grace for his size, he offers it to his mate who throws it down her gullet. Then she feeds him, and back and forth they go. Somewhere here lurks a lesson for fragile human relationships.

It is inevitable that I follow the hornbills, in a wooden dingy used by forest guards for patrolling the park. Armed guards accompany me too, and even though the park's bloody history stays in my mind, the gun appears intrusive in this spectacular landscape. The boat gives itself up to the rhythm of the river, lolling and swirling as it follows the waves. The waters of both countries unite, in utter disregard of international boundaries, like the birds above. Two huge, pointed horns, attached to a bulky wild buffalo, poke out of the river.

The boat wedges itself on the bank and I step on Royal Bhutanese soil. I need no passport, no one questions my credentials. A placid army of foresters greet me, and over a cup of *lal chai* I feed their curiosity. No, I am not a scientist, not a government official either. Here, I am but a child of nature, smitten by her beauty and curious to explore her wonders. They wave me inside, nature is no one's property: it belongs to everyone.

A few steps later, I meet my fellow avian travellers, dozens of Great Hornbills. Most lovingly feeding their mates, while others forage for themselves. A few doze, nestled against the crook of the huge *Bandardima* tree, their heavy heads dipping forward, like old men unwittingly falling asleep in their armchairs.

I am dwarfed amidst tall trees rising out of flowering shrubs. Perched on them are the animals that have brought me here, the Golden Langurs, found only in this tiny patch of the earth. These blond beauties, and the commoner and drabber langurs back home, are all part of the same family; the former being the most glamorous member of the clan.

They are a huge group, well over two dozen, and I settle down on a fallen log, my eyes and lens fixed on the primates above. The langurs reciprocate my curiosity, a particularly bold member fixes his beady eyes on me, his tiny black face framed with tufts of fur smoothing down to a golden coat. A few assorted pairs diligently groom each other, combing and parting their blond hair. Essential to the beauty regime, I assume, when blessed with such luscious tresses.

My attention shifts to a tiny simian nestled at her mother's breast. I gather it is the baby of the family, surrounded by a cache of adoring aunts. One hugs her close, then another takes over, carefully cradling her in her arms. She is handed back and forth between clearly smitten adults, but oh-so-carefully. Why do we humans assume that we are the only ones blessed with emotion? That we are 'higher' beings because we can feel, while other animals live in a sterile world. I tear myself away, exceedingly unwillingly as the pelts of the langurs glow gold in the morning light. I wonder if this

Golden Langur

The KING and I

Royal Palace, Manas, Bhutan

paradise can be my permanent abode, the only option is the very charming summer palace of the King of Bhutan. I still await the invite.

That Manas thrives today, we owe to its rag-tag army of foresters. Ritesh Bhattacharjee, deputy director of the park, told me that in the last six years, eleven of their men have been killed. He took me to Bansbari, a shattered skeleton of a forest *chowki*. It had been razed to the ground, only the charred and stunted walls remained. Guards were slaughtered and the department elephants shot to death. That was February 1989. On the same morning, all the anti-poaching camps within the park were attacked. The militants were well-armed and flush with money, the guards had rustic, non-functional guns. The forest staff were not trained for guerilla warfare, nor were they equipped with automatic weapons, to counter the mines and explosives being used against them. Many were killed, and morale was at its lowest.

'Militants destroyed everything in this park. They finished off the rhinos. There were numerous tuskers, but all killed for their ivory. I patrol Manas, every day, but it's been a year since I have seen tuskers,' rues forest guard Babulal Oraon. He has been our shadow for the past two days, a rusty .315 rifle slung over his shoulder. It's not an antique showpiece purely for effect. It's a weapon he has used repeatedly and brutally against the enemies of the park. In his career he has had over a 100 encounters and killed 32 poachers. Once he was badly injured and beaten up by the hunters, but battered and injured, he fought on, delivering them to justice. For years, he faced a death threat and still thanks the unknown face who risked his life to save him. The late Prime Minister Indira Gandhi decorated him for his courage. He has not fought the battle alone: there are others who maintain a lonely and risky vigil. Underpaid, indeed sometimes unpaid. All uncertain of their tomorrows.

Their efforts have paid off. The rhinos, once locally extinct, are back. Hoof prints have been seen. Rhinos have a habit of defecating at the same spot and there are reports of dung heaps and big ones at that. Which is good news, indicating that there is more than one rhino using the common lavatory.

Now, the battle is over, and the enemies of yore have joined hands. Ex-poachers, foresters, militants bonded by the love of Manas, work towards its protection. It is to uncover this story of poachers turning over a new leaf that I went to the eastern side of the park. This particular visit has taken months of meticulous planning with letters, faxes, mails going back and forth, peppered with doubts and reciprocal reassurances.

For years, Kokilabari has been no man's land, laid siege by Bodos, a rebel tribal group fighting for their own land. For years, the forest was ravaged, its animals slaughtered mercilessly. But now the Bodos are protecting the animals they once shot, allegedly to partially fund their movement. Under the aegis of Mauzigendri Eastern Manas Eco-Tourism Society, conserving Manas and promoting it as a tourist destination is a goal aimed towards earning an alternate income.

I am the first honoured guest, the army soldiers at the checkpost are astounded at my arrival. Tourist, they mutter disbelievingly but graciously wave me in. We bump along roads designed to induce the worst backache and are frantically waved down by Bodo women. Repeatedly, I am pulled down from the car, luminous eyes gaze at me in wonder, tentative hands smooth down my hair, bolder ones pinch my cheeks. Initially, I am alarmed at the assault, but it dawns on me that it is an intense curiosity that drives them, the joy at being confronted by an outsider. To me their beauty, wrapped in hand-woven *dokhnas* and filigree jewellery is exotic, and I guess they reciprocate the feeling for me, a creature oddly adorned in ragged jeans and pulled down by assorted cameras. As soon as I arrive at the modest tourist home, the women break into a dance. Each movement has a meaning, each graceful turn conveys a message. They throw their arms wide open to welcome a guest and wave swords to fight the enemy.

Pygmy Hog

The KING and I

I am particularly entranced by the fire dance in which women swallow the flames. Throughout the dance, the fire is used as a metaphor for anger and how it is a destructive force. In the end the anger, or fire, is quelled. The dance takes on a special intent, as a metaphor of the bitter battle against Manas and its denizens that has finally met its end.

Next morning, I enter the jungle, riding on an elephant.

Leopard Cat

I feel like an ancient explorer, stepping on territory hitherto unknown to man. My thighs ache as I sit astride the bulky giant, but I can vouch that there is no better vehicle for jungle roads. The great animal sways beneath us to a uniform rhythm. Seated twelve-feet above ground I enjoy a vantage view of what lies beneath, and the Capped Langurs hollering above us seem closer as well. A wild boar hurtles itself at our striding pachyderm, snorting derisively. I am not surprised at this mismatched battle, the boar is a plucky creature, known to even take on a tiger. Having made its presence felt, it departs, followed soon after by a dwarfed version. This is not a piglet, but the Pygmy Hog, yet another creature endemic to this park.

A few hours later, I meet Budhesar Bora, a diminutive man packed in a wiry frame. His eyes sparkle and a smile steals over his serious countenance ever so often, dimpling his cheeks. We are perched on a fallen log in Tanganmara amidst elephant dung deposited minutes before. Two years ago, the tusker wouldn't have passed by, unconcerned and unharmed. One shot from the *gaazimara*, the Bodo name for the locally produced gun, and the mighty giant would have toppled. His tusks would have been chopped off and sold across the border in Bhutan, at Rs 3,300 per kilogram.

Killing the elephant comes easy to Budhesar and by his own admission he has slaughtered eighty. He bagged two tigers; of deer he has lost count. The prize though was *Kurusu* or the Greater One-horned Rhinoceros. The hunters would go in a group, about a dozen of them, sometimes more, tracking the animal in the forest. To find one took them many weary days, rampant massacre had put an end to the season of plenty. 'For the horn,' says Budhesar, 'I usually got Rs 1.7 lakhs.' When it reaches the ultimate customer, the costs multiply manifold, thanks to the misguided notion that the matted hair that constitutes the horn, serves as a magic elixir for impotency. Joysaran, another ex-poacher takes me to the Khwisifurhri waterhole. He points to the water, the real elixir of life, where animals came to quench their thirst. It made killing easy, all the poachers had to do was wait patiently for the unsuspecting creatures in scorching summers. He had been party to a rhino hunt here —

Bodo Woman

Budhesar Bora

perhaps the last of them, a few years ago. The killing was indiscriminate, voluminous. With lawlessness ruling, other unsavoury elements had joined the fray. The forest became a killing field, flowing with rivers of blood.

He has given up the gun, they all have after February 2003 when a new settlement was signed for the creation of Bodoland. It goes beyond a surrender of violence: the Bodos are actively protecting and managing the park. Twenty-seven Bodos patrol the park round the clock and, last heard, had seized a cache of over seventy guns. Budhesar did his bit, too. Stationed at his rickety watchtower in Tanganmara, he nabbed seven men armed with sophisticated weapons. The society has built roads for better patrolling and has started grassland management, burning tracts of old grass before the monsoon so that the fresh showers will allow the new shoots to grow. This is a vital tool in grassland management as new grasses attract herbivores and with a healthy deer population, carnivores and other animals too will flourish and breed.

This jungle is not just a jungle; it is a miracle. The Miracle of Manas. How else do you explain trigger-happy poachers and terrorists now fiercely protecting the sanctuary? Or bitter enemies joining forces to cherish the park? Budhesar terms 'his' park extra-special; the day before, Babulal, the forest guard had called it his paradise. I agree.

I must leave Manas, but Manas will never leave me.

The Lion in his Winter

Ten thousand years ago, Asiatic Lions ruled the wilds from the Mediterranean to India. They now cling precariously to an impossibly small domain. Gir National Park in Gujarat is their only home on planet earth, false pride and a misplaced sense of ownership prevents us from giving them another. With just over 300 survivors, it is a rare privilege to see this majestic animal. It is to the lion that I owe what my friends term as my 'big-cat hang up'.

Gir

The Asiatic Lion was the first big cat I saw, captive and wild, both within an hour. I was then nine and it was my first trip to the jungle. My acquaintance with animals was minimal, we didn't have pets and those were the days before *Discovery* and *National Geographic* channels had brought wildlife into the bedroom. My first sight, before we entered the precincts of the sanctuary, was a lion trapped in a tiny metal cage. He was exhibited to us with much flourish: Behold the mighty beast tamed by man! He was a recent catch, and the forest officers recalled with much relish how difficult a job it was to capture the ferocious animal, even though the lion was past his prime. His canines had dulled, his gait had slowed and he had taken to preying on the village cows. The villagers were incensed and the lion was subsequently trapped after an effort of ten days. I looked at the beast pacing frantically in his prison, his twisted, restless movements constrained by lack of space. He stepped forward, then backwards, then forward, and backwards. Again and again and again, his emaciated body taut with restrained effort. Then he let an anguished roar emerge from deep within. I stared, aghast, at the trapped animal, unable to look him in the eye. I was free, his freedom had been barred. He was to be shifted to the zoo nearby. The king of beasts would become a Sunday amusement. I don't think I introspected much back then, but I do remember feeling what I can now define as a sense of injustice. A certainty that a cage was no place for a wild animal. I then and there resolved never to visit a zoo, a promise I have kept ever since.

An hour later, we were in Gir, standing in the thorny scrub jungle staring at a lion sprawled not ten feet away from us. There were no fences here, and the lion was in his domain. He appeared unconcerned at our proximity and I took a step closer. Only a tiny step but enough to arouse the lion; he roared. Massively. Terrifyingly. I scrambled back to safety. His roar was potent with wild rage; how dare I invade his territory? A far cry from the tortured call of his captive cousin.

Though I did not quite recognise it then, the lion became the first big cat to bite my conscience and sensitise me to their plight. Even today, I bristle at what I see as the 'Cinderella' treatment to the Asiatic lion. I perceive it as the spurned royal heir being denied its rightful kingdom and confined to a consolatory patch, a tiny fragment of the land that the 'Lion King' once inhabited. The African lion, with its larger mane and numbers, has almost erased its Indian sibling from international consciousness, and back home, the star of the show is undoubtedly the tiger.

The KING and I

Top: Jam Sahib Shri Dilipsinhji on shikar 1940
Below: Viceroy Lord Linlithgow 1942

But it was not always so, the lion has always been the symbol of supreme dominion and enjoys a glorious history, while its journey down conservation lane is chequered and replete with interesting anecdotes. Once it reigned supreme, commanding a range from Persia to Central India. For the Mughals, the lion was the ultimate trophy, and Sir Thomas Roe observed, 'that no man may meddle with the lion but the king.' Emperor Jehangir killed over 50 lions in his impressive massacre of 28,532 animals in a lifetime! The French traveller Bernier records that 'it is considered a favourable omen when the king kills a lion, the termination of an unsuccessful hunt invites evil to the state'.

While researching old shikar records, I read records of lion hunts in Mathura. Mughal Emperor Akbar came across a pride of seven there; if you went to Mathura now, you would be lucky to spot a cat! Aurangzeb put his son Sultan Mauzzam's strength to test by ordering him to attack and kill one. Delhi, that impossible urban jungle where I now live, was once, with its scrub forests, an ideal lion habitat. Here's one for the records: Emperor Jehangir details his encounters with the lion at Palam, the site of the international airport in the capital, in *Padshahnama*. After the Mughals, Maharajas and the British continued the destruction. One imperial officer, Colonel George Acland Smith claimed to have shot 300, fifty of which were in the neighbourhood of Delhi. William Fraser eliminated eighty-four around Haryana and Punjab, while Raja Bishen Singh of Bundi in Rajasthan bagged over a hundred heads.

The massacre took its toll and by the end of the eighteenth century the lion was under severe threat, eliminated from all its territories save a tiny patch of forest in Kathiawar. Here too, the hunt was on. In two separate hunts in the same period ninety-four lions were slaughtered. By the turn of the next century, the lion was in dire straits. Rampant hunting coupled with large-scale conversion of forest into agricultural land had forced the animal into virtual extinction. It was the Nawab of Junagadh, an ardent animal lover, who came to the rescue. The lion also found an unlikely saviour in the then Viceroy, Lord Curzon. It is said only about a dozen lions remained in Gir in the beginning of nineteenth century, though there are those who allege that the Nawab deliberately lowered the figure to detract royal hunters and sahibs whom he couldn't otherwise refuse. The ruse worked. Wrote the Viceroy in a letter urging their protection, 'Up until the time of the mutiny lions were shot in central India. They are now confined to the ever-narrowing patch of forest in Kathiawar. I was on the verge of contributing to their still further reduction a year ago myself but fortunately found out my mistake in time, and was able to adopt a restrain that I hope others will follow'.

Nawab Mohabbat Khanji III, an eccentric animal lover, passionately protected the lions. The Nawab's love for animals is legendary. He was clearly besotted by his canines, whose marriages were elaborate ceremonies befitting any royal union, complete with *baraat*, nautch girls and feasts. For three days during the wedding, a state holiday was declared. I visited the Nawab's palace in Chorwad, a village by the sea, the chosen venue for the canine weddings. The palace is now a shattered ruin, but Raji, a woman who sells the sweetest coconut water at the beach, tells me that the ghosts of the wedded canine couple still haunt the beaches and terrorise those unkind to dogs. At Partition, the Nawab abdicated and left for Pakistan. As the story goes, he only took with him half of his wives but all his dogs!

A rough census at the time of independence shows about 250 lions, and the numbers are now stable at about 350; the 2005 census quotes 359. With such a minuscule gene pool, the Asiatic lion qualifies as the most endangered big cat in India. Paradoxically, it's odd to think of the *Panthera leo persica* as threatened, for Gir has as many lions as it can hold, and more. The forest cover is thick and the jungle is bursting at the seams with lions. Gir is proving too small for the big cats and it is a problem of plenty. With territory in short supply – a male can command upto 200 kilometres – over 65 lions have moved out of the sanctuary, and 20 among these actually live on the beach.

Nawab Rasul Khanji of Junagarh, 1855-1911

Mohabbat Khanji, the last Nawab of Junagarh, 1900-1959

The KING and I

A lioness on the beach, Saurashtra coast

My most spectacular leonine encounter was not strictly at Gir either, but a few miles short of Diu, a coastal town about a hundred miles from the park. A Maldhari waved, motioning us to stop our car. I figured he wanted a lift. Certainly, I did not expect what happened next. We parked the car, and I got down to investigate, when a low growl from behind froze my blood. Slowly, I turned my head and not too far away crouched a lion: an enormous male, his head framed by a magnificent mane. I gaped in shock into the lion's unflinching eyes, too petrified to make a move.

The moment was broken by a low, rumbling moan from across the field and the lion turned and disappeared. I recovered enough to shift my gaze to trace the lion's movements — a golden blur gliding through the green — as it unhurriedly ambled towards the female, waiting at the other end of the farm. In the same field, a couple of farmers nonchalantly

Maldhari

Siddi women selling *jamun*

continued their job of plucking cotton even as the king of beasts strolled by. '*Tame sinh nathi joyu? Tamhe beekh nathi lagti?* Doesn't the lion scare you?' I asked. The men shrugged; lions were part of their life, though earlier confined to the jungles, they now had strayed to many surrounding villages. To date, they had not attacked man. So people were not really scared. But yes, the lions fed off their cows, and that was a problem. Livestock was their livelihood and they really could not afford to lose cattle. Then, they went back to their work, and while I admired their resilience, I wondered how long it would last.

I had a similar meeting with the Maldharis inside the park. Maldharis are professional graziers, as native to Gir as the lions, and have lived together since time immemorial. '*Aavo ben,*' Ismailbhai hails me as I cross his *ness* or cluster of huts. Ismailbhai offers me freshly churned *chaas* or buttermilk and regales me with many a lion tale, his favourite being that of Dharam and Veer, named after a big Indian blockbuster, *Dharamveer*. Just like the *filmi* heroes, these two were fearless and romanced many a lady. Curiously, as on celluloid, the two worked as a team, hunting together, fighting off other males. Somewhat unusual for a species where the women are said to bring in the daily bread! Then locals poisoned Veer, and Dharam just lost the will to live, Ismailbhai says with a sigh. Such romanticism has stood the Maldhari-lion relationship in good stead but the conflict between the neighbours is steadily on the rise. Maldhari buffaloes are an essential ingredient on the lion's menu, and though thorns fence in the bovines, the felines have learnt to circumvent them. It is an inevitability the Maldharis live with.

Says Kanubhai, another shepherd, '*Sawaj to amari sarkar chhe, ame ene van ma rahieye to e tax to leve, das taka,*' (the lion is like the government, we live in their land so they take the buffalo as tax, about ten per cent of our cattle). But this tolerance is fraying and the villagers are retaliating against their livelihood losses. In the last three years over sixty lions died, an

The KING and I

unusually high number. Forest officials maintain that most are natural deaths, but the unpalatable truth is irate farmers, avenging their cattle being lifted, have poisoned a considerable number. In one case in Dhari, a neighbouring village, a lioness died after consuming a dead buffalo, which had been sprayed with insecticide.

To survive, the lion has to contend with other factors, not the least of which is the problem of acute inbreeding, which have made the beast something of a genetic monster prone to disease. Worse, it has led to sperm retardation, implying that in the long run a baby boom is an impossible dream. As it is, perpetuating the species is no easy task, the big cats have to copulate no less than 500 times to produce a litter.

The most serious threat is undoubtedly the fear of an outbreak of a disease that could wipe out the entire population. It is not a doomsday prediction. In 1994, canine distemper killed more than a third of Africa's Serengeti lions, a fate that can easily befall their feline cousins in Gir. Relocation of part of the population is called for. Gujarat disagrees, the lions are theirs, they claim, and this is where they will live. And die.

Gir for me has always provoked mixed feelings: a sense of wonder at this wild paradise islanded in a state pillaged by industrialisation and relentless development, and a sense of despair at the grim future of the beast that portrays the emblem of India. Each leonine encounter is a moment of both joy and despair. I saw a pride once, a mother with her two cubs and an 'aunt' a little further away. They were lounging atop some rocks, their bellies bulky with a recent meal. The adults dozed, legs up in the air while the cubs frolicked. It was a peaceful scene but the calm appeared deceptive, given the threats looming over the lion today. I looked over at the lion pride and wondered. Did Simba, the lion king, have a future?

In Search of Sher Khan

Melghat Tiger Reserve is in Maharashtra, one of India's most industrialised states. Melghat was my first foray into the land of the tiger. No dramatic encounters, just the overpowering aura of the sovereign of the forest. Tigers are the soul of the jungle, omnipresent, affecting the colour and character of the landscape. The local tribals, the Korkus, who pray to Baghdevta or the Tiger God, say that the tiger must never be slighted, always revered, never feared, always respected. Then, you will be blessed.

I was a novice when I visited Melghat; this was my first foray into tiger country, and my first feel of the intangible, yet all-pervading power of the tiger. I did not see the tiger in Melghat, but it was here that I learnt my most important wild lesson, a mantra I still live by. Seeing the tiger was not essential to the itinerary, it was a bonus. I knew that even if I did not see it, it was aware of my presence. I exalt in this knowledge till today. Even in its presumed absence, the tiger makes its presence felt. It is there in the sudden nervous darts of a frightened doe, its perked-up tail stiffening with alarm, in the stamping of its leg, in the raucous call of the peacock, in the air that suddenly stands still, fraught and tense, as though waiting for death to strike.

The KING and I

Forest Spotted Owlet

Melghat does justice to its name 'where the *ghats* or hills meet'. As we curve up the slope towards Melghat, the mountains are covered with a canopy of white flowers and the air becomes heavy with the syrupy scent of the blooming sal. A befitting welcome to the land of the tiger, more so than the tacky board that announces the same.

I visited Melghat in the winter for just a day. I had been warned that I could forget sighting tigers. It's a big forest with rolling hills, deep valleys and thick foliage, assisting the tiger in its right to privacy. Besides, it was winter, when sightings were rare. Water, and therefore food was well-scattered, not concentrated in few and fixed places like in the summer, forcing the predator out in the open. Incidentally, the Park director had been posted in the reserve for six years and hadn't seen one.

We drove into the deep forest. Rocks and trees on the wayside bore the legendary family planning advice diligently doled out by the government, *Hum do hamare do*. Whom was the government targeting here in the heart of the jungle? When last heard, animals didn't read, and wouldn't we rather that tigers and other creatures have more kids anyway? Kishore stopped my inane banter right there, and pointed instead to more relevant matters, big hoof prints embossed deep in the wet mud, telling us that a herd of bulky animals had passed this way some hours ago. They were of the gaur, often referred to as the Indian bison; it was the only sign of their presence that I was to witness, if I discounted the ageing trophy mounted atop the dining table at the forest resthouse. The latter had stared balefully at me as I sat beneath it, prompting me to shift base outside. We disembarked, tracing the movement of the gaurs and decided to take a short – really short – walk in the forest. I confess it is against the rules to walk in the tiger's domain. Isn't safe, either. But we did it anyway.

We were walking up a *kucha* path with a water hole just below us we when heard a langur bark, echoed by its mates. The cheetal stamped an agitated foot, repeatedly, then let out a high-pitched, creaky call. Over the years, as my trips to the forest become more frequent, the jungle's *lingua franca* becomes familiar. It was the prey warning others that the predator was here. It was the prey letting the tiger know that it was aware of its presence, thus taking away the element of the surprise attack, essential to a successful hunt.

Back then, it was the experienced Kishore who pressed my hand in warning, Be quiet, be alert, be careful. We walked a few steps ahead, letting the sounds lead us on. My breath was caught in my throat, dry with a nervous excitement. I knew – we knew – that moving towards the carnivore was not the wisest act, but it was an unseen force that propelled us forward. Then, as suddenly as the panic had erupted, it eroded into a deceptive calm.

We cautiously made our way back to the jeep. And, there, surrounding our Gypsy, were pugmarks, so fresh that the dust was yet to settle. Huge, squarish imprints indicating that it was a male. Yeah, yeah, I muttered. We had missed the tiger. By seconds. I looked around frantically, not a blade moved, not a sound heard. The pugmarks had disappeared into the dense undergrowth. While we had gone looking for the big cat, it had come looking for us, giving our vehicle the once over before proceeding with its business. The air was heavy with a pungent cat smell. I bent down to touch the hollowed, hallowed sand, yet warm from the stealth of the tiger. I did not need to see it – him. He was here. And from that moment on, my life changed, divided into two parts: BT and AT: Before Tiger and After Tiger.

On the way back I spotted a cheetal fawn. It was tiny, barely a few days old. Its eyes bulged in terror, appearing disproportionately larger than usual. It was alone, which was unusual, for mothers rarely leave their young alone and unprotected. I worried and fretted. Why was it alone? Was it lost? Where was the mother? Has the mama deer, God forbid, been killed by predators? Would this fawn, vulnerable in its solitude, fall prey to a wandering tiger? Very unscientific, my concern, I was aware of the law of nature, but heaven help me, it was beyond me to think of the tiny fawn as just a link in the food chain. Kishore wisely drove away before I launched into some unwarranted, foolish rescue act.

We spent the night at Semadoah. The forest guesthouse at Semadoah would certainly lose some points for luxury, but it is superior to any five-star as far as location was concerned, overlooking the River

Sipna and fringed by the Vidarbha hills. Decadence in a forest is out of place, here one lives with Mother Earth, communes with nature. The gaur head glared down at me, filling me with guilt for being human, the same species that reduced him into a trophy. I moved outside. Lovely, I thought as I positioned myself under a tree of indeterminate identity. Who needed Einstein's brainwave? God had provided us moonlight, and a gentle breeze. And snakes, one of which lands, *platt*, on my plate. I screamed, Kishore jumped, the cook ran askew, and one very bewildered snake slid away. Non-poisonous, Kishore reassured. Didn't do much to my ruined appetite and I called it quits for the night. Spent in the verandah, with stars and mosquitoes keeping me company.

Next day, I shifted focus from the tiger. I was keen to meet the Korku tribals and to go on an owl hunt for the rather drab-looking Forest Spotted Owlet. For one so small, it had created quite a racket in the ornithological world by its unexpected reappearance from the nether world. It was a great story. A bird, presumed dead and thought extinct for 113 years, suddenly brought to life in Melghat.

I had to see this other, well-known, denizen of the Melghat forests. Kishore, who had been screaming for a long while, well before the official rediscovery, in 1997, by Pam Rasmussen, that he had seen and indeed photographed it. He was rightly miffed at not having got the true credit for the rediscovery. He put his angst behind him and we set off to look for this diminutive nine-inch bird that so closely resembles its more common cousin, the Spotted Owlet. We trudged through several miles of forest, Kishore confidently leading the way. He knew his forest well and that special nook which hides this special bird. He pointed to the branches where my eyes could discern nothing, till what appeared to be wood took on a rounded shape. I cannot describe the pleasure of this moment, of watching a bird thought to be extinct back to the world of the living. I must add here, that it was with much glee that I, later, crossed out this species from my *Encyclopedia of Vanished Species*.

I stopped at Tarubanda, a small Korku village, inside the reserve. The Korkus have been living within the Melghat forests, they were brought here by the British some 200 years ago as labour to cut the teak or *sagwan* trees for railway track sleepers. What a terrible contradiction for the Korkus, who are ardent worshippers of nature. They venerate the tiger

Rusty Spotted Cat

The KING and I

and welcome him into the fields for he is the God of fertility and will guarantee a good harvest. The Korkus have built a hut for the tiger to 'stay' lest it ventures too close. Since human and livestock fatality is rare, I gather that the predator abides by these maxims by and large. They bow to the gaur and the hills as well, and there are deities for small pox and cholera, though all of the above are invariably inferior to the sun and moon Gods. Unfortunately, the passage of time is eroding such reverance.

The Korkus make a potent brew from the flower of the *mahua*. To my eternal regret, it was not the season for the *mahua* flower. My eagerness to make its acquaintance was provoked by Captain J Forsyth in the *Highlands of Central India* who wrote that the 'spirit when well made and mellowed by age, is by no means of despicable quality'.

I sat with the women, and they chatted about their life in a forest. Their fields were regularly uprooted by wild boar or the *sukhdi*, and the villagers took turns for all-night vigils to drive away the vermin. There were other problems: their population was growing and so was their need for roads and education, but once a road cuts through a forest, it spells doom, as it brings with it unplanned development. The plan to shift the villages outside the park has been on the anvil for years, and recently a few villages were successfully shifted out.

The topic shifted to more personal matters. I was intrigued by their way of life, and they by mine. The kitchen was engulfed with smoke from the *chullah*, and tears streamed down my cheeks. The women laughed, but not unkindly. How do you cook then, they inquired? And what? Who did I cook for? Myself. Laughter, again. Even more uproarious. Not for a man? They told me that marriage was fairly early in their society, and the father of the bride was usually paid a substantial amount, plus a sari as bride price, for here it is usually the woman who bears the burden of life. The price climbed higher if the woman in question was easy on the eye, and more importantly, a hard worker.

I could see they could not comprehend my single status. Shakuntala, whom I have become quite friendly with offered a solution. 'Why don't you stay here?' she suggested. 'I will pay your father Rs 5,000 and give your mother a sari.' Seeing the shock on my face, she reassured me pointing to gaudy filmi posters lining the wall, 'Don't worry, my son looks just like Sunil Shetty!' For a split second, no longer, I was sorely tempted, seduced by a world sans deadlines and blessed with natural beauty. I looked at Shakuntala, touched by the serious intent and eagerness shining in her eyes. How incredible were these people, in a matter of hours, they had welcomed me into their home, and heart. Even promised me a secure tomorrow, a permanent abode in their future. It was with no little measure of regret that I fumbled my excuses and walked away from my first formal marriage proposal. Then the Sunil Shetty bit hit me. Our film stars turn up everywhere, even in the tiniest village in the remotest areas, such is the power of Bollywood. I wonder if the nice Mr Shetty knows that he has a look-alike lurking somewhere in the heart of the tiger's terrain?

Jackal

Born Free

Bandipur Tiger Reserve, in Karnataka, forms part of a contagious, though increasingly fragmented, forests of Mudumalai in Tamil Nadu and Wayanad in Kerala. Like many other protected areas, Bandipur was once the royal hunting ground of the rulers of Mysore in south India. My tryst, too, had royal connections. Vishalakshi Devi is the sister of the present Maharaja. Times have changed. Hunters of yore are passionate conservationists today. Visha is a gentle soul, passionately devoted to animals. Little wonder then that she and her equally enthusiastic husband, Nanu, are frequently anointed caretakers of Bandipur's wild orphans, Bambi, the lost deer, Prithviraj, the impish pachyderm and Baby, the leopard to name a few. It was the latter that piqued my interest, an orphaned cub nurtured by people and rehabilitated back to the wild. Critics point out that a human-raised carnivore cannot thrive in the wild and may turn man-eater, owing to its familiarity with man. 'Baby' now nursing her third litter has proven her detractors wrong.

It's called fey; this calm before the storm, the ecstasy before the agony, the sheer delight that precedes impending disaster. It was destined to happen. My heavenly interlude cannot be attributed, in entirety, to the fact that I was at the edge of the Bandipur Tiger Reserve, a much needed fix for a die-hard wildlife addict, though if truth be told the reserve had a pivotal role to play. The nightmare that followed my visit lacked the romance of an encounter with the notorious forest brigand Veerappan (he was slain in a dramatic encounter three years after my visit). Instead, I owe my misfortune to an ordinary thief who wiped out in one single, effective blow all the photographic evidence of my stay in the Garden of Eden, otherwise called Tusker Trails.

Tusker Trails is a wildlife resort with deceptively simple cottages, set amidst lush greenery and a log hut that serves as a dining hall, not unlike other such resorts that cater to tourist traffic in India's wildlife hotspots. What sets it apart from its brethren is the people who own it. Or should I say the animals who have taken over the resort as their natural home?

The KING and I

This tale veers away from the average wildlife traveller's histrionic moments of close encounters with potentially dangerous animals like tigers and tuskers. If I were to liken this story to a book I would call it *Animal Farm*, or modify Gerald Durrell's classic to *Their Family and other Animals*. Or Joy Adamson's immortal tales of Elsa, the lioness who was *Born Free*. On second thoughts, Tusker Trails is the perfect cocktail of the above three, smoothly blended to provide a heady mixture of a royal family and their entourage of leopards, elephants and deer. The resort is the brainchild of the blue-blooded Gajendra Singh Auwa and Vishalakshi Devi. The former belongs to the kingdom of Auwa, while she descends from the royal family of Mysore.

It was raining hard as I drove down to Bandipur from Bangalore, though the rain gods simmered down as the car drove into Tusker Trails. My visit was preceded, indeed spurred on, by the extraordinary story of orphaned elephants presently occupying a rather large guest enclosure of the resort. But nothing had prepared me for the reception I was to receive. A curious trunk, shot out at me, halting my ascent to the reception. The trunk came attached to a baby elephant, though from my viewpoint there was nothing 'baby' about him. He was huge, at two years he weighed ten of me, and this sudden encounter made me shriek. The calf bellowed and then marched determinedly after this peculiar, hysterical arrival, me. What followed was utter chaos, soon brought to a peaceful halt after I hurriedly emptied my bags off all things edible and into the bottomless pit called Prithviraj. But that was before I learnt that there were two more eager mouths to feed, Padmaja and Padmini, making an utterly charming and inconceivably naughty gang of three orphan elephant calves, who have made this resort their home.

Bandipur

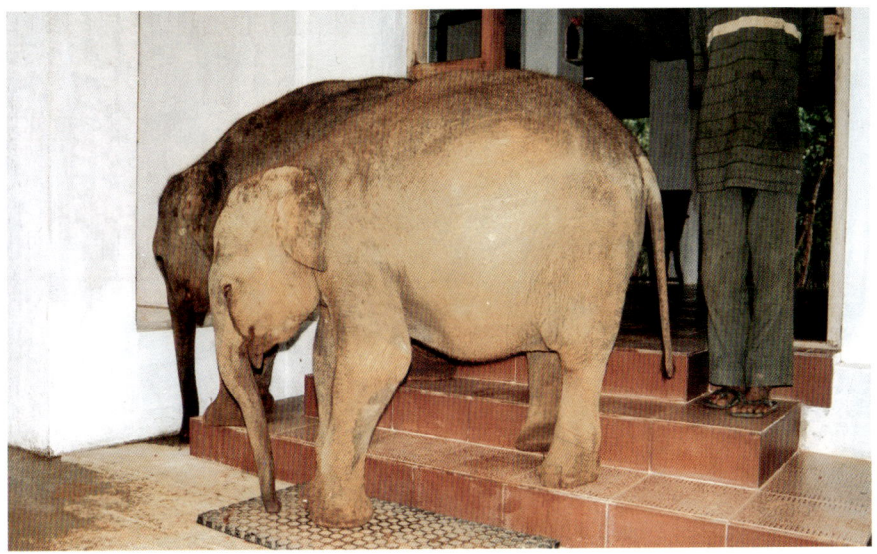

Prithviraj and gang

This isn't usual, Rudrapratap, the Auwa heir assures me, just that the rains had put a halt to the calves' routine romp to the pond and nearby woods. Instead, the pachyderm gang chose to investigate the newly built reception area. No complaints, wayward elephant at the reception counter are more my thing than the impeccably polite variety at hotels.

A refreshing hot bath followed by the house specialty; cold coffee and an appetising meal later, I joined Nanu (Gajendra Singh) and the boys for a game of cricket. A few minutes into the game, indignant bellows emanated from Prithviraj who interrupted us. This, said Gaj Singh, was a complaint being registered for starting the game without him. Prithviraj, like any quintessential Indian, was a cricket maniac and boisterously joined the game. My camera clicked furiously as the pachyderm determinedly studied his friend's movements and made a quick run between the wickets. Prithviraj was agile for his size, careful not to topple the men and wickets that stood in his way.

Fun time over, the elephants noisily made their way to their meal, and we to ours. Over a quiet drink I learnt that the happy family picture hid a tragic past, their presence at Tusker Trails told of a deep ecological crisis that looms over the survival of Asian elephants, not just in India but in other habitats where they exist. Padmaja's herd had ventured into agricultural fields that were once the ancient migratory routes of elephants. Her mother was electrocuted by a faulty electric fence, designed to emit mild shocks to keep marauding elephants away. Padmaja's little trunk was singed as well, and forest officials discovered her suckling away at her dead mother. Prithviraj fell into an elephant-proof trench when his herd was being driven away by angry farmers from their fields. Padmini has a similar story too. To claim that the elephants were traumatised would be an understatement. Prithviraj would trumpet into

The KING and I

the night, unable to eat and sleep and Visha remembered spending nights hugging him to sleep. He would run towards anything green, squeaking frantically, relating his mother to the green of the forests.

Early next morning, I ventured into the tiger reserve. Game was thin, the rains had dispersed the animals further inside the jungle, explained our guide. Still I came across huge herds of cheetal. I saw the Malabar Giant Squirrel, brilliant orange and brown leaping from one branch to another, like a graceful Russian acrobat. Prithviraj's family in the wild escaped me, but a herd of gaurs crossed our path. The gaur's 1000-pound bulk tapering down to white socks gives the animal the air of a well-muscled schoolboy, who has suddenly sprouted a pair of horns. I caught a glimps of the fox. We headed home, welcomed by a hot breakfast and the incessant trumpets of Padmaja & Co. I dropped by to say hello, only to be whacked by a petulant Padmini for adventuring on my own. Prithviraj made for my camera, as usual, a contraption he was fascinated with.

The elephants, however, were by far not the only animals that these royals had been entrusted with by the forest department. I reflected about Bully and Baby as we drove towards the jungle around mid-morning, overwhelmed by the story of the two leopards, nurtured by humans before being released to the wild. They were found in a sugarcane field. It is a matter of grave concern that leopards are increasingly using sugarcane fields — this has been seen in Junnar in Maharashtra and Junagadh in Gujarat — and tea gardens in eastern India, as 'nurseries' as forests and natural habitats give way to agriculture. The mother may have gone hunting when the villagers found the cubs, or more insidiously, she may have been poisoned. The forest department entrusted their care to Tusker Trails. The cubs arrived at the Tusker Trail doorstep late one night in a crudely woven plastic bag, usually used by villagers to carry provisions. The cubs were

Previous page: Baby, the Leopard; Left: Cheetal; below: Indian Fox; right: Gaur

tiny, 'so tiny, they could have fit into my beer mug,' recalls Nanu. Their eyes though open were covered by a blue film, they couldn't see and looked utterly helpless.

Nanu says it was love at first sight. 'My first thought was "Wow", so entranced by their beauty was I,' says Nanu. His delight gave way to despondency and a fierce determination to give them back their rightful home. 'They shouldn't be in a shopping bag. They don't deserve this, these orphaned cubs. They were creatures of the wild, denied their mother by man. By us,' he remembers thinking. He was determined that they would go back to their true home, the forest. Ignorant in the way of wild cats, the family pored over Joy Adams' books and urgently wrote to Billy Arjan Singh, who pioneered such an effort before in India, 'We are lost. We know it is a very loose question but can you kindly guide us by telling us the do's and dont's in the matter of bringing of leopard cubs?'

The cubs' growing up is a story that calls for a book in itself. How does one put it succinctly in one short para, the love and devotion lavished on the cubs by the Tusker Trails family, their triumph in nurturing an alien species as their own and the struggle to maintain an emotional distance as they prepared Bully and Baby for their eventual return to the wild?

Bringing up the cubs had all the joy and heartbreak that nurturing your own child entails, added with the extra care that orphaned animals require. Frequent feeds by milk bottles, soothing an ill or traumatised cub. They often erred, cows' milk, they learnt, didn't agree with cats so they shifted to Esbilac, a formula feed for babies. Each detail was meticulously noted, down to the colour and amount of stool passed. Discipline was important, too, more so for Bully, who was at the receiving end of more than the occasional whack. 'He just couldn't keep out of mischief,' recalls an indulgent Visha. I went through

The KING and I

Parakeet chicks

their detailed diary, thoroughly enthralled by the antics of the cubs, wishing desperately that I had been part of it. Bully was, well, typical boy — naughty, brash and an irrepressible show-off. He plunged into everything without a second thought. Nanu insists that children cross the species barrier, and one particularly endearing note convinced me of that. 'April 23, 1998, Bully is down under with a bout of colic, shows lameness in the leg and is unable to bear the weight of his forelimbs. Everyone felt sorry for the poor, ailing cub. He was carried everywhere and generally made a fuss of'. Bully loved the attention and the royal treatment. This, he thought, was the life. So even as he got better, he put on the air of a martyr, faking a limb injury so that he was still carried around like an aging, pompous Maharajah. The game was up however, when he spied his sister playing with Pratap and the other kids. Bully's natural exuberance took over and he rushed in to join the romp, quite forgetting that he was feigning an illness!

Baby was the opposite, one could sense her thinking things through, carefully applying her mind to the problem and then making her attack. It was this ability, believes Visha, that helped her survive in the wild.

For the first few months, Visha was imprisoned to the resort. Bully and Baby were convinced she was their mother and clutched on to her. If she had to go away, her *duppatta* stayed behind, its reassuring smell would soothe the cubs' plaintive cries. As they grew up, the cubs were put in a separate enclosure and taught to hunt live food. Twenty months later, the little spotted balls of fur were full-grown carnivores. It was time to for them to leave. 'It broke our hearts, but it was the only way, leopards are wild creatures. Bully and Baby were entrusted in our care only till a time they could survive in the forest,' asserts Nanu. Nor would the couple recommend rehabilitation as an answer to problem of orphaned babies of poached mothers. 'It cannot be the answer at large. Individually too, it is very risky and if in the wrong hands, it could manifest into a horror story. It requires total commitment, someone who is willing to write off a number of years. The leopards have to be priority. In our case, they took over our lives and everything else took a backseat. One did what was best for them, not us. Every minute I took care of them was geared towards their eventual freedom. We loved Bully and Baby but they were never pets,' muses Visha.

Still, it is a moving tale of mutual respect, and love, across species. The leopards, considered the most effective killing machine among big cats, never left a scratch on them.

Or that when back in the wild, Baby let them into her inner circle, even interrupting her mating once, much to the considerable annoyance of her mate to meet her human friends. She has granted them the occasional privilege of watching her litter of cubs. She warned them of the presence of a tiger nearby and once took on the ferocity of a matriarch elephant charging towards a hapless Visha. Bully's freedom died young, one month after being rehabilitated in Bandipur, he was gored to death by a sambhar. Baby pined for her brother before her natural resilience and survival instincts took over.

Now I was on my way to meet Baby, to be included in this inner circle, though my position was that of a spectator on the periphery. I followed the leopard men: Rudrapratap with helper Doraiswamy in another, enclosed jeep, since familiarising Baby with strange humans is not concurrent with her wild instincts.

We reached Baby's territory and Doraiswamy called out, *Baby, Babywa, Babyyyywaaaa.* Come, Baby, Come. My heart behaved strangely, thumping loudly before almost standing still. Leopards in the wild are a rare enough sight; this one is a carnivore of both worlds. Reared by, and fiercely loyal to her human family, Baby is nonetheless a creature of the wild, hunting, mating and rearing her litter of cubs. My heart dipped with every passing minute, panicking that Baby will deny me. Thirty minutes later, we are ready to turn back when she appeared. Her movements are guarded; she had scented a stranger but once reassured Baby threw caution to the winds.

The scene had a surreal air. I was almost convinced that the animal rubbing her head affectionately against her foster parents was a house cat with hyperactive growth hormones,

The KING and I

Spotted Owlet

Hanuman Langur

were it not for the golden glow of her skin or the power packed muscles of her sleek body. I could see her canines, sharp enough to rip people apart, a powerful blow would make her human family history. But this was not to be. Animals do not forget so easily.

Her tail twisted indicating excitement, as she encircled her people. They belonged to a different world now, but the links remained. Baby leapt gracefully into the Gyspy sniffing out the little chicken she knew was meant for her before bounding out again. She was a child again, pampered and playful, it was only her swollen teats, which reminded me that she was a wild leopard. Baby was a mother, thrice over. So captivated was I with the drama unfolding before me that the camera almost lay forgotten. But the mind, and the heart remembered. We turned to go away, Baby gave one last look, her golden eyes mesmerising, before she walked away towards a wild future, and freedom.

The Tusker Trail menagerie houses much more than elephants and leopards. There was Bambi the cheetal stag, separated from his herd. He attached himself to a herd of goats and was brought over by the shepherd who thought Bambi would make a good meal for the leopards. Visha thought otherwise and Bambi stayed in an enclosure built specially for him. Once mature, he left on his own but drops in occasionally with his harem to renew the ties. Dogs come with the package too; my favourite is Boogiemari meaning the child of Boogie, a pie dog who lost his leg fighting off a wild boar. Her mournful looks and servile ways are part of a careful design to win a place in your heart, and some morsels off your plate. Boogiemari holds her own with the elephants as well, occasionally joining them for play, quite unmindful of size differences.

It was my last night and I snuggled in, my ears attuned to the trumpet of the elephants but today I heard another call. It was a langur giving sharp alarm calls. He was persistent, warning us of a predator nearby. A leopard, possibly. Baby? No, I was told later, Baby doesn't visit her childhood home anymore.

I bid goodbye to the family and their animals, with Prithviraj making one last desperate attempt to lunge at my camera. Considering that I was to lose all my captured moments later anyway, I might as well have gifted him the camera. I would rather have a delighted Prithviraj, than a happy thief.

The Killing Fields

I salute the Leopard. It is an incredible cat, beautifully draped in its spotted golden coat. Its compact frame packs immense power and an agile mind. Unfortunately, all these qualities that it is endowed with have condemned it. We skin it because we want its fur to drape our shoulders, we harvest its bones for irrational cures, we have killed its prey, we have stoned it to death when it enters our habitation, under duress, since we have destroyed its home. The leopard is a survivor, it fights back, adapting skillfully to a new, harsher environment. Conversely, these survival skills prove costly, throwing it into direct conflict with man. A battle it is fast losing. Panthera pardus is yet another cat on the death row. Unnoticed and unmourned. Forgive me for not telling a pretty story. But almost all my shared moments are tinged with tragedy — lifeless skins, a cache of bones, bitter, gruesome tales of killer leopards and of a free, wild spirit captured in cages.

Rudraprayag is a prominent feature in India's spiritual map. If you were to follow the pilgrim's path, your holy trail begins at Haridwar in India's northern state of Uttranchal, where the devout converge for a ritual dip in the *ghats*. With the sacred River Ganga by your side, you can soon reach Rishikesh, where you may pay homage at the Laxman Jhula, the precarious rope bridge suspended across the holy waters. The bridge, now resurrected, was supposedly built by Lord Ram's brother, Laxman with the help of Lord Hanuman's monkey army. The simians are still at large on the bridge, though they lack the self-control of a disciplined army. It would be well-advised to keep your eatables well-hidden from their opportunistic eye. The road, accompanied by the holy Ganga, climbs higher along the Kumaon slopes till it reaches, many miles later, Srinagar, the former capital of Garhwal, a town that has long overgrown its charm. Devotees then determinedly proceed on the arduous climb to Badrinath and Kedarnath, but I am a pilgrim with a different quest.

The KING and I

Ram Singh Negi

My journey's end was at Rudraprayag, situated at the confluence of the rivers Alaknanda and Mandakini, which now flow as one to meet the Bhagirathi at Karnaprayag. This holy town earned disrepute as the region under siege by the infamous man-eater of Rudraprayag, put to an end by the legendary hunter Jim Corbett, but only after many spine-chilling encounters.

The road to Rudraprayag is heavy with traffic, bus, jeeps, cars bearing pilgrims tear down the road, belching obnoxious fumes and it seems improbable that this was once the nocturnal haunt of the legendry man-eater. But that was in 1926, and I was here eighty years later, revisiting history, attempting to find answers to the unnerving puzzle of man-eating leopards. Why had the tragedy not abated? Why do the killings continue, down the years and across the country? Were leopards instinctively man-eaters? Or was the leopard killing man, as Corbett concluded, for its own survival?

As in the days gone by, Rudraprayag still sells itself as a religious destination. *Dhabas* flank each side of the road, offering the pilgrim sustenance for their arduous journey; savoury stuffed *paranthas* with sharp piquant pickle and piping, hot *chai*, all on the cheap.

Gulabrai, three miles short of Rudraprayag, is a modest hamlet. It bears scant testimony of the fact that the man-eater met its end here, barring an aging tree with a machan gloomily stranded in the middle. This was the mango tree where Corbett spent many cold and terror-filled nights in the pursuit of the man-eater. An ancient witness to the end of a gruesome episode. In its shade below a plaque has been constructed: *On this very spot was killed the man-eating leopard of Rudraprayag by Jim*

Corbett on 2 May 1926. The leopard, in its eight-year career, had killed 125 humans and ensured that no man knew safe passage while it lived. Yet as it lay dead at Corbett's feet, he felt no triumph. Satisfaction at ending the terror of the town, maybe, but coupled with a naked poignancy at ending the life of a magnificent animal.

As he wrote, 'Here was only an old leopard, the best hated and most feared animal in all India, whose only crime — not against the laws of nature but against the laws of man — was that he had shed blood with no object of terrorising man but only in order that he might live'.

Across the wall was a hostelry set apart from the rest by its nomenclature which clings to the Corbett legacy. Suresh Deol owner, beckoned me to Leopard Inn. Young Suresh was clearly budding Corbett enthusiast. A lone aficionado around these parts, he was relieved to find someone who shared his interest. From a drawer, he pulled out a carefully conserved, well-thumbed copy of *The Man-Eating Leopard of Rudraprayag*, opening it at page 150. He had highlighted parts that mentioned the 'pundit who owned a pilgrim shelter' and with whom Corbett was well-acquainted. In Corbett's words, 'In addition to the many interesting tales he had to tell about the man-eater, he was only one of the two people who survived an encounter with the man-eater'.

The KING and I

T. N. Deoly, the pundit's descendant, was not short of tales, either. He was justifiably proud of his great grandfather, 'who kicked the terror of the town in his verandah and lived to tell the tale.' Suresh guided me to the old pilgrim shelter, now so debilitated there seemed little hope of its revival. Suresh, however, was resolute to build the house to attract Corbett addicts. He was determined to market the hunter's legacy, which he feared was fading with time.

I also found Corbett in the dim memory of Ram Singh Negi, a Second World War veteran. He couldn't fathom my impulse to revisit the past, so many decades after the event but obliged with the little nuggets he can remember. Negi was just fifteen when the leopard came calling and he recalls the terror well. It was not a mere animal, he recollects, but a strange evil spirit, with the body of a beast but the soul and mind of a man. The logic that ruled, in those days, was that the leopard was too crafty, too intelligent for an animal. He was *narsimha*, half man-half animal. It would carry just the body away, leaving the head behind as though severed off with a sword. It came only at night, when the village slept. If you kept vigil in the front of the house, it slunk in from the rear, if both the doors were guarded, there was always the window.

It was befitting that Rudraprayag marked the beginning of my leopard trail. Unfortunately so, for all its beauty and grace, the Prince of Cats is primarily viewed as a problem animal. Back then, Corbett maintained that it was old age, wounds and stress of circumstances that drove an animal to kill man. The Rudraprayag leopard is an example, it had suffered bullet wounds too, dating back to the year he turned man-eater.

The situation is much worse now, with man destroying the leopard's habitat and reducing its prey base and thereby throwing man and leopard in sharp conflict. The prince has been reduced to a pest. Menace is the word bandied about. Nothing really has changed since Corbett's time, we are still wrestling with the problem, which has become more severe over the years. History is repeating itself, and we haven't learnt any lessons. Rudraprayag, and indeed Gulabrai, are freed of the terror now but it forms part of the Pauri-Garhwal region, where on an average thirty-four people are killed annually by the leopard.

The occurrence of the man-eater, however, is spread across India. In Mumbai, the leopards of Borivli National Park slayed 11 people in 2004 bringing the financial and glamour capital of India on its knees. The city that never slept locked itself in at seven, lest terror should strike. Just over a hundred kilometres away to the north-west lies, what a report in an English Daily referred to as, 'the killing fields of Junnar'. The spotted predator had killed nine people in the years 2001-2002. In desperation, the forest department began trapping the animal on an unprecedented scale. So much so, that the Junnar forest division appealed to be admitted into the Guinness Book of Records for capturing the maximum number of leopards! When last heard the figure was 102, and climbing. In Gujarat, they showed me a 'fatality map', fifteen people killed in Baria in South Gujarat in 2003-2004, a superintendent of police was killed by a mob that had collected to kill a guilty leopard. Junagadh had six casualties, the cat had mauled over a dozen people in Vadodrara district. There are instances of leopard attacks in Jammu. In Chandigarh, a leopard walked into a house, settled himself on a sofa in the drawing room. The TV was on and probably bored by the programme, went into a fitful sleep to the horror of the family that returned to find the carnivore in peaceful slumber in their house.

The human face of the tragedy is immense, but there is another side of the story. The story that explores the root cause why leopards turn man-eater.

Essentially, the leopard is a shy, solitary animal, and now a rare sight in the wild. Not being the top predator, like the tiger or the lion, it lives on the fringes of the forest and villages, surviving on small game like cheetal, barking deer, wild boar, langur and in times of

The KING and I

Top: Hunters kill a 'man-eating' leopard; above: Poachers with leopard skins

scarcity even frogs and hare. A burgeoning human population, expanding agriculture and development projects have destroyed and severely degraded India's forests. The leopard's habitat has given way to human habitation, forcing this reticent predator into the open. The law has banned killing for meat, but the taste for exotic flesh and the urge to hunt has decimated cheetal, barking deer and other venison that form the leopard's natural diet. Naturalists say that the leopard is a survivor, the most adaptable of all cats and will eke out a living in the toughest of conditions.

Ironically, this adaptability has become its bane. Homeless and starving, the leopard has been forced to stray into villages, which were once forests, for food. Dogs are a favourite. The leopard will target chicken, goats and if all else fails, man. When cat mauls man, quite understandably, people bay for its blood. They kill the beast in revenge, stone it to death, hack it to pieces, burn it to ashes. Sometimes for man-eating, occasionally for preying on their goats or simply for blundering into human territory. Recently a colleague filmed a horrifying sequence of a leopard being set on fire after it had strayed into a village in Uttar Pradesh. There was no history of man-eating or even cattle kills here, it was fear that lit the fire. One particular vision remains fixed in my mind, of a photograph taken near Bhopal in Madhya Pradesh that captured a leopard hanging upside down from a tree. It's leg was caught in a trap set by local farmers to poach deer for the pot, but a leopard walked into the snare instead. As the cat frantically tried to free itself, it only managed to get itself more entrenched. When it tried to escape by jumping, it just got more entangled in the tree and the branches pulled its tail higher, until it hung upside down, like a condemned goat before its slaughter. The photograph caught the agony of the animal, its eyes bulging with pain and immense misery, but it is not that what haunts me. It was the crowd of onlookers, easily a thousand of them, gathered there to enjoy the spectacle. They were laughing. Laughing. That people could look on, not in sympathy and concern but feel some inexplicable glee at the pain of a tormented creature was something I could not assimilate. This was not even a direct experience, yet it was a defining moment in my life. It drove home to me, more than the cold statistics of number of leopards poached, that the leopard was doomed.

Not all leopards are man-eaters, yet in the quest for revenge, many innocent leopards become victims. There is no dearth of instances when man-eaters are used as an excuse to go on a hunting spree. As soon as a fatality comes to notice, a death warrant is issued for the man-eater. Hunters indulge in catfights to grab the license to kill. To appease the bloodthirsty public, the first animal that crosses their path dies. If it turns out to be the wrong animal, another one goes. This method of 'trial and error' has actually bred man-eaters. More often than not, bad shots injure the animal, and once wounded the leopard resorts to easier prey, like man. Even in these days of ecological enlightenment, it is still macho to bag a big cat trophy. There are resorts in certain areas that still offer hunting as the ultimate thrill for very select clients, and the top prize is the leopard.

What will drive the final nail in the leopard's coffin is the demand for its skin and bones. The skin lends itself well to the garment industry, and there flourishes an underground market for its dappled skin. Should you walk the streets of Lhasa and other places in Tibet, you could easily buy a leopard skin coat off the shelf.

We do not know how many leopards survive today. There are no authentic census figures of the leopard and estimates vary between a dismal 7,000 to an optimistic 15,000. Perhaps we can hazard a guess by counting the dead. For every tiger skin seized, ten of the leopard are hauled. Experts estimate that around 500 leopards are slain

Villagers with slain leopard

every year. In the year 2000, the massacre was at its zenith, over 1,300 were slain. In 2004, a seizure in Tibet yielded 579 leopard skins — all from India. In April 2005, forty-five skins were seized in Delhi.

There is little doubt that the leopard is endangered. A note circulated in the Ministry of Environment and Forests expressed the fear that it is declining faster than the tiger, there is no telling which one will go down first in this macabre race.

Sadly, the morbid man-animal conflict has ensured the leopard has no supporters, no impassioned conservationists taking up its cause. Public opinion has not rallied around for the leopard. And protecting it from poaching is a task near impossible, even if there were a will to combat it. There are no designated reserves unlike that of the tiger where forces can be deployed to counter poaching, though we are yet unable to do the same for tiger reserves.

Solutions, however difficult they are, must be worked out to minimise conflict. Where there is good prey base, say Bandipur and Gir, cases of human mortality are almost nil, making it a good model for conservation to build on. Unless a massive effort is initiated to resurrect buffer zones and fringe forests and end the decimation of its prey base, there is little hope for the Prince of Cats.

Leopard caught in a trap near Bhopal

Just One Tiger

Palamau is the only tiger reserve in Jharkhand. Part of the Chota Nagpur plateau, it was once a verdant forest, teeming with wildlife – tigers, elephants, gaur and the ill-fated cheetah. Game has thinned, largely due to widespread hunting over the years. The district gazetteer of the late nineteenth century records the reward for eliminating 'pests:' Rs 25 for tigers, Rs 5 for leopards. The tiger faces other, equally insidious, threats today. The MCC, an extremist group, uses the park as its base, making patrolling and management risky business. Fragmentation has segregated the tiger population. The result? The tourist zone of Betla has just one tigress living in a desolate world, deprived of a mate and motherhood. Long after my return from Palamau, the doomed fate of the lonely tigress, haunts me.

'Only one piece', is the answer I get when I, and other hopefuls, ask the inevitable question at Betla, the tourist zone of Palamau Tiger Reserve: How many tigers? The notice board at the guesthouse announces the luck of one 'Happy Mr. S. Bonrji & party' (I assume it was Mr. Bannerjee, though happy at seeing the big cat, might have been a little aggrieved to see his name misspelt) who saw the tiger last, precisely forty days ago. Not a chance of a feline encounter, but it wasn't this missed opportunity that had me depressed. I hope, but never presume, to see the tiger in its designated reserve. Just the thought that they live and thrive; that we are neighbours; if only for a fleeting moment in time, that I share their territory, has me content and happy.

My anguish stems from the fact that Palamau, and indeed this entire Chota Nagpur green belt, once had a problem of plenty. Now this glorious tiger history has whittled down to *just one piece*. Sir John Houlton, who wrote *Bihar, the Heart of India* in 1949, speaks of his incredible experience of seeing five tigers together. 'I was amazed to see five large tigers walk out of the forest opposite me and begin to cross the river. They were a huge male tiger, an old female and three two-year-old cubs. My shot killed the old female; one of the other guns dropped a cub in the river. The others followed their sire to safety'. Remarkable, and I do not only mean the incredible sight of five tigers, Sir Houlton's record could well be the first of spotting a tiger family. Tigers are solitary animals, though of late there has been speculation that they are sticking together in times of stress. Rarer still was the notion of male bonding, father and sons strolling down for a drink, for males are often known to kill even their own cubs, in fear of future competition.

Left: Fort at Betla; above: Tribals at the weekly *Haat*

The KING and I

At that time, the tiger had a price on its head, dead or alive. It wasn't only the desire for a trophy that decimated the numbers; cubs were captured live for the local gentry as they made a regal addition to the menagerie. Palamau was a fertile ground to feed this trade for live cubs. Cub-catching here reached epidemic proportions, Balakrishna Sheshadri recalls in his book, *The Twilight of India's Wildlife*, 1939 that a batch of five cubs was sold at a mere Rs 15 a piece at the Daltonganj Court, the town where the headquarters of Palamau Tiger Reserve is based now. Times have changed, threats remain constant. Live trade in cubs has ceased, only to be replaced by a maniacal demand for their skin and bones.

There are other worries too. The forest provides a base for Naxalites, an ultra-leftist guerrilla group. Their violent presence in the jungle has made vast tracts of the forest inaccessible to forest officials. They protect the forest putting their lives at risk, not knowing if they will return home. If the jungle gives life, it also hides lethal land mines. Like the one that blew up a forest jeep in 1998 killing two of their men. The following year, a ranger was abducted. In 2004, a land mine wrecked a jeep, killing two trackers, their dismembered bodies strewn in the vegetation. In between, many others were martyred for the cause of Palamau. Tusks stolen from the nature center, officers assaulted, homes set on fire. But by far the most horrifying story is the case of a forest officer who raided a village, Dorami and recovered cheetal meat. He was surrounded by a huge, enraged mob, compelling him to open fire. A life was lost. In revenge, the heads of two trackers were chopped off. One was slaughtered, even as his little daughter clung on to her dying father.

Besides the MCC, other militant factions and plain-old fashioned dacoits have moved in, who loot at gunpoint. Palamau is a wealthy forest, rich in teak and *khair (Acacia catechu)*, which goes into the making of *paan* and *gutkha*, an indigenous addictive. Illegal smuggling of these has caused tremendous unrest. How, I wonder, do we protect tigers in such a savage land? Hazaribagh, the land of a thousand tigers, preceded my trip to Palamau. The name has inspired a raging dispute. One school of thought insists that the town is Hazaribaug, christened after a certain Mr Hazari, a farmer of considerable means. His sprawling mango orchards were used by the British as camping grounds when on the march from Calcutta to Benaras. The British referred to the place as 'Hazari's baug,' or Hazari's garden, and so the name stuck. Motilal, a wizened old forest guard, prefers to think of this as the land of a thousand tigers, for the forests were once tiger wealthy. He squats before me, an ancient green warrior, his wise eyes peering intently into a vacant forest. The same eyes that had once rejoiced at the sight of the tiger, now search in vain. Motilal is one of the few who has seen the tiger in Hazaribagh.

Wild Boar

The KING and I

'I saw the last tiger here,' he proclaims. When? Doesn't know. Some *hadiya*, the potent, local rice beer, and his memory serves him better. 'It was with Sahi Sahib when I saw him, standing a few feet away. He was beautiful. The tiger, not the sahib,' he chortles, his eyes crinkling in delight. Motilal is referring to S. P. Sahi, a legendary forest officer. Today, mines have ravaged the sanctuary, pressing in from all sides, scarring the earth, destroying the water. A national highway, a constant carrier of trucks loaded with coal, cuts through the heart of the forest. Eighty villages live in and around Hazaribagh, seven have made the core area their home. Cattle roam freely, eating the grasses, inhibiting regeneration. The MCC lives here, too. They had warned the forest guards not to wear their khaki uniform, lest they be mistaken for the police, their main target. What chance, then, did the animals have? Was this how we defined a sanctuary, a protected area? Hazaribagh, the land of a thousand tigers. Call it what you will now, the tiger count is down to nil. Local extinction is a reality, not a doomsday theory by vociferous conservationists.

I spend the next day walking through the forest, looking for tiger signs, looking for miracles. A futile exercise in a sterile forest. No tiger could possibly exist in a land pillaged by mines, devoid of prey and degraded by man. My gaze hungered for any animal, any signs to show that this was a sanctuary. The only animal I encounter is a cheetal, closeted in a wire enclosure. She walks staidly to the wire, her nose twitching in anticipation for a meal, periodically doled out by indulgent, ill-advised tourists. The only sign that this is tiger country are the decaying remains of a trap designed to hunt the beast built by the former ruler, Padmaraja. When the Maharaja hunted, the cat was lured into this trap, a sort of well covered by foliage, and with bait stuck in the middle to fool the misguided tiger. Hazaribagh manages to retain its beauty, nature's resilience has ensured verdant greens, natural lakes and the presence of some small animals. But the forest leaves me horrified. A terrifying vision of our national parks of the future. Is this the fate of our sanctuaries: Hunting traps reminiscent of splendid tiger country and deer enclosed in wire to reassure that there once were animals?

Grey Mongoose

It is in this gloomy frame of mind that I enter Betla. I wander into the bazaar, the tourist zone is a village and has a myriad of shops offering Chow Mien and STD facilities to visiting tourists. I am looking for mineral water. They don't have it, but a helpful trader offers liquor instead, from the finest scotch to a local brand called *Jhatka*. I am sure such a weird priority points at some social malaise, but my mind is preoccupied with the job at hand, trailing the only, lonely tiger.

Palamau

Sambhar

Whether the quarry is met or not, the hunt is always pleasurable. It is bitterly cold at 6 am, as I climb Juhi, the elephant and let her lead me into the jungle. She is prettier than her Bollywood namesake and trots headlong into the forest, lithe and nimble for an animal of that size. I hear a faint slither just behind us. Snake? And drop my bag, promptly retrieved by Juhi. She is usually obedient, but grunts in protest when nudged by her mahout, Imamuddin Ansari, as she crunches on bamboo. Her reaction to bamboo is typical of a child in a candy store. She spots one, squeals in delight and rushes headlong to grab chunks of this delicacy. Munching from one end and dropping from another, she plods on happily into the territory of the lone tigress of the region. I have little hope of seeing the queen of the jungle when the langurs on tiger duty bark in alarm, incessantly, sparking off terrifying calls by the peacock. A herd of cheetal, completely hidden till now, pours out of the foliage and rush off in a stampede. The denizens of the jungle are on a red alert. I wait. Tense. Eager. Breathless. Desperate. But it is a 'no-show'. Royalty does not deign to present itself to all its subjects and I, clearly, am not the chosen one. Seconds later, the air and the potential tiger prey around us relax. She has moved on. Imamuddin shakes his head sadly. Once this was a healthy jungle, rich with tigers and prey. Rare was the visitor who left disappointed. His eyes mist as he talks about Nawab, the dominant male. '*Memsaab, uska raaj tha*,' he says, waving his hand madly to indicate the vast dense jungle around us, 'all this was all his territory.' He prattles on about the former king, gently prodding the elephant along and I realise how intimately woven is his life and that of the animals he protects.

The KING and I

We, sitting in a cocooned world of the urban metropolis, may make passionate speeches on the importance of conserving endangered species. But it is Imamuddin, and others like him, who are the real earth heroes, who live with the animals, follow their movements, rejoice in their well-being, feel their pain and mourn their passing.

Chastened, we head back to the guesthouse, after a mandatory pause at the bamboo candy store. I climb down, and in a rare gesture of affection, Juhi touches her trunk to mine. Nose, that is. At dusk, we gather around the fire as the cook expertly whips up *chappati* fresh from the clay tandoor. Also present is 'Tiger Reporter' Mohammed Umar. As his designation implies, he is appointed by the forest department to doggedly follow the tiger. He has been doing this for two decades, dutifully noting down the minutest detail from the birth dates to the number of cubs to the colour and quantum of tiger crap. His day starts at 4 am, and long after the sun has set, he scouts for pugmarks, scats, spoors, scratches and any other sign of the lone tigress. His work is dangerous, patrolling the forest, day and night, alone with only a *lathi* for protection.

Worrisome though they are, Naxals are far from Umar's mind; he is worried about the curious predicament of the single tigress. He is after all, the 'father of an unmarried daughter', and one destined to remain so. As if on cue, I hear a faint call, *aaaouumm aaoumm....* Continual. Insistent. Unanswered. Here is my encounter with the tiger. Unseen, but heard. Here is proof that the tiger lives on at Palamau. But only just. There is no echo of my delight in Mohammed; he sinks further into despair, enveloped into a grief so private and profound that it is scary. 'Don't you understand, Rani is calling for a mate.' He hears her desolate call, night after night. Rani is nearly seven, if nature had her way, she could well be ready for her third litter now.

Indian Muntjac

I am told there is a male in Chippadohar, the neighbouring range, that a railway line cutting through prevents Rani and him meeting, mating. I know it's a busy line, 60 trains ply through this forest route everyday. I know it is a fatal development, a dozen elephants have been mowed down in recent years. Still, I doubt the story. Nothing, not even a killer train would keep the tiger away from a female in heat. I doubt a tiger exists at all next door. But the fact remains, wildlife and development do not mix, if we dream of a healthy, viable tiger population, perhaps we could give the animal priority in his reserve. Just one tigress. Denied its maternal instincts. Destined to die a spinster. Not sentimental drivel but the reality of Betla's tragedy. The 2005-census officially has put the tiger population of about thirty-six to forty, a number that is strongly disputed in non-official circles. It is hard not to be sceptical. I hope it's true, I fear it isn't. I hope too, that these are not isolated tigers in a fragmented Palamau. Like Rani.

Given the park's bloody record, it's a wonder that the forest survives. That there is still life. A cheetal that balances itself on two feet to reach the tender leaf, the magnificent gaur who laps at the water unsettled by our jeep, the mongoose who runs awry at the scent of humans. I marvel, too, at the resilience of the foresters who stay on, despite all odds and under the threat of the gun.

So many murders, so much arson, but like many others in the forest department, tracker Salim Ansari labours on, undeterred. He is a delightful character and an ardent devotee of Rani. He feels a certain responsibility. After all, he brought her up, sort off, after her mother, Begum was killed. Poisoned, most likely. Rani and the other male cub had to be fed artificially. Live baits were tethered for a year till the cubs learned to fend for themselves. The male has disappeared since. It's years since Ansari has taken leave, gone to his village. 'Rani,'

Blue Bull

The KING and I

Author with park elephant

he says in all innocence, 'won't like it.'

Next morning, I use the car for a jungle safari. A meeting with Juhi's wild cousins lifts me out my disappointment of missing out on my elephant vehicle. The Gods are kind today. Five minutes into the park and I spot an elephant some feet away. The giant moves, slightly, to reveal a tiny, tiny calf suckling away urgently at mama. I look on as she hurriedly provides cover to the baby, and makes a curious gurgling call, summoning her kin. In seconds, from within the green cover, an army of no less than a dozen assorted 'aunty' elephants and sub-adults emerge and form a protective circle around the calf. They keep a beady eye on me, alert for an untoward movement. I stand still, easing into a silent truce where both pledge to keep their distance. I watch baby suckling, mama crunching on tree bark, constantly touching, communicating, reassuring each other with their trunks. I feel privileged to be part of such a tender moment of a truly wild animal, when this elephantine paradise is shattered by an obnoxious group of tourists who rush headlong into this intimate family scene, honking loudly. Their vehicle, a battered ambassador stuffed with innumerable heads and limbs, spews toxic fumes and the bodies inside squeak in mortal terror, *Haathi*...

The peace is lost, bedlam breaks loose as the pachyderms squeal and trumpet in panic. Luckily, the noisy gang hurtles on, leaving behind an agitated herd in its wake. Our truce vanishes; clearly, now, I am one of 'them' — the enemy (and ashamed to be so). I hold my ground refusing to move away in the face of a potential risk. The flustered mother bellows and charges head on towards the car. Had she been serious, the car and its passengers would have been history. But such is the generosity of these magnificent creatures that she halts, abruptly. Barely six inches away, she stops, glares as though communicating a silent warning and walks away, dignity in every step she takes.

I think of the louts in the ambassador making faces and yelling at the pachyderms, and I think of the matriarch and her dignified retreat. Need I say who walked away with the honours? I thank her silently and turn back to my home for the day, the forest resthouse.

Elephants do not find mention in old records of Palamau. There are different views of how they came to be here. One says that these are the descendants of the elephant army of the

Chero dynasty whose fort still stands in Betla. Once the king lost his kingdom, the animals were
turned loose in the forests and became feral. Another story explains that the animals have wandered over from across the border in Chhattisgarh. As habitats shrink the elephants seek new pastures, and these have found succour in Palamau, at least for the time being.

My next destination is Netarhat. On the way I halt at Barsamand, in the heart of the reserve. The forest officer accompanying me describes this as an essential gastronomical pause, offering the best *kalakand*, a sort of milk cake thickened into cream. I bit into the fleshy sweet, it melts at the first touch. Eatopia is interrupted by a sharp iron object, almost lost in the mud, that catches my eye.

A careful examination reveals nearly a dozen bullets, casually scattered on the forest floor. There had been an encounter with militants just two days ago. The conservator shrugs, struggling to appear unfazed. This is the reality of Palamau, designated tiger reserve. This is the war that he and the tiger fight every day.

This would have been the end of the Palamau chapter but for a tragic epilogue. I visit the park a year later in 2005. Tiger tracker Mohammed Umar is no more. He died in the forest. Killed by elephant? Killed by illicit fellers? Killed by Naxals? Who knows? He was alone, and the dead tell no tales.

The Grey Ghost

I stood, chilled to the bone, surrounded by valleys and mountains of ice, my lungs unaccustomed to the sparse air, my eyes unacquainted with such stark beauty. I was 13,000 feet above the sea on the ancient grounds of the Hemis National Park. It is a blessed region, sacred for its antiquated monastery and abounding in rare natural wealth. This is the realm of the Snow Leopard, the most beautiful and elusive predator that has walked the earth. Knowledge of the Panthera Uncia is as scarce as the animal. Science can only guess that 5,000 remain, spread thinly across five million square kilometres of the remotest mountains of Central Asia.

That the Snow Leopard is, that it is here, that its frosty eyes watch us from the mountains, that is enough.
Peter Matthiessen

Mission Impossible: A quick trip into the rugged Himalayas to find the snow leopard and come back with glorious photographs and tales of exciting cat encounters. I stare at the editor in horror, trying to reason that snow leopards do not present themselves by appointment or comprehend deadlines. I had six days to plan my trip, venture into the oxygen-starved climes of the Himalayas and hunt for the predator. Successfully, of course. It was hysterical, impossible and futile. I am glad I was foolish enough to take the plunge.

The KING and I

The start is especially discouraging. People well acquainted with the cat are skeptical, to say the least. There aren't any 'likely' leopard sighting spots. The snow leopard is a very rare, wild sight. Wiser men have spent cold, lonely days, months hoping to spot the big cat. All in vain. Even the villagers who share its habitat have lived, and died, without ever sighting the snow leopard. They know it's there. The *shen* is a regular visitor to their villages for a meal, killing their goats and sheep. They say it's a ghost, the grey ghost of the mountains.

My hunting ground is the Hemis National Park, just twelve kilometres away from Leh in Ladakh and one of the best-protected habitats of the animal. The sanctuary earns its name from the ancient Hemis Monastery dating back to AD 1672, though regretfully I have to give it a miss in pursuit of my feline goal.

Panthera uncia is a true blue MNA: a Multi-National Animal occupying the snowy lofts of Central Asia: Kazakhstan, Tajikistan, Kyrgyzstan, Uzbekistan, Mongolia, Tibet, China's Sichuan and Quinghai, the Hindu Kush and Karakoram in Pakistan and through the Himalayan and trans-Himalayan regions of India, Nepal and Bhutan. The leopard occurs along the border areas of Russia with China and Mongolia and is usually found above the tree-line cover of 3,000 metres. Its wide distribution is not indicative of its density. Populations are so sparse and local estimates so uncertain that no one knows how many wild snow leopards survive. What we do know is not very encouraging, there are barely five thousand of these animals left, and declining.

The flight to Leh is at an unearthly hour and since it flies to border-sensitive regions, it is bogged down by strict security regulations. It's bitterly cold, but well worth it. In precisely fifty-seven minutes flying time, I sight the mighty K2, glide by the mythical Nangaparbat, fly over the Amarnath Shrine and skirt the frozen battlefield of Siachen. I am at a position of distinct advantage, lording over the mighty Himalayas, looking down at lofty peaks as I sail through the clouds. Soon, the tables will be turned and I will be reduced to a tiny speck exploring the mountains from ground zero, seeking the mystical monarch of the snows.

Leh, ground zero for Mission Snow Leopard, brings me back to earth. First, there is no room for me, and the photographer Alwin Singh. It is off-season; most hotels display a closed sign. The few guesthouses that do exist are for some obscure reason reluctant to offer us single rooms. All my efforts in Snow Views, Mountain Top, Snow Heaven etc. are met with giggles and nudges, and sidelong glances. Imbeciles, I mutter unkindly and change my strategy, adorning the garb of a wronged woman. This man is horrible, I appeal to the weathered old woman. We-had-a-fight; he-beat-me kind of thing. She shakes her head in understanding, glares at the unsuspecting photographer, puts a reassuring arm around me and guides me to my room; larger and nicer than what Alwin gets. Poor man, for the remainder of the stay I am indulged while he gets a raw deal.

The second setback is illness. I had been warned: For the first two days lie on your back and play dead, or that is what I would be. Leh is at a height of over 11,000 feet, above the tree line, and a period of acclimatisation is essential for everyone ascending from the plains. I didn't pay heed, rushing around various offices, talking to scientists, and NGOs, organising transport, getting permits and other paraphernalia required to get to Hemis. More fool me. I lie on the bed in sheer misery. The simple task of getting up is near impossible. A mere step leaves me fighting for breath and my head hurts so terribly that I beg Alwin to cut it off just to escape the terrible pain.

The assorted forest officers whose support I have enlisted in the search for the elusive leopard frequent my sickbed. They come, shake their heads, make sympathetic noises and advise me to go back. Or at best, to visit the beautiful ancient monasteries the region is famous for. I stubbornly stick to my goal. Listening to advice was never one of my strong points.

My first sight of the snow leopard is a dead one. It is a pelt of the animal carefully stored in a musty room of the headquarters of the wildlife department of Ladakh. The smoky grey fur dappled with black rosettes is soft to the touch. I wonder sadly if this will be my only encounter with the snow

The KING and I

leopard. This beautiful relic of the dead species haunts me, for the pelt, which shields the animal from harsh winters and is perfect camouflage to fool its prey, is also its biggest enemy. Its fur is the ultimate, if clandestine, fashion statement in the west, much sought after and priced higher than that of the tiger. A snow leopard skin coat is softer, warmer and drapes better. The skin had been recovered on its way to Delhi, an important centre for wildlife trade. One paw was missing, the leg poignantly ending in a bloody mass. Evidently, it was entrenched in a trap. The horror of it chilled me to the bone. I could feel the creature's bewilderment as it tried to break free, I could imagine its agonising cry as the jaws of death cut deeper and deeper into its leg. I could hear the haunting wail of the leopard as it must have starved and bled to death.

The locals here are Buddhists and the non-violence preached by their religion has conserved the species, though protection is wearing thin by the exorbitant price it earns the hard-pressed nomads. I am shaken by this deathly encounter, but it spurs me on to seek the snow leopard, alive. I have been in Leh for three days and no closer to the animal. I look out of my window at the snowy peaks of the Himalayan range. Somewhere, out there, is the grey ghost of the mountains, and I need to find him. How, when and where… I do not know.

Till I meet my saviour, Rinchen Wangchuk, a hardy young man and the Indian arm of the Snow Leopard Conservancy, an NGO dedicated to its continued protection. Rinchen does not give me false hope, but understands my desperation for a feline encounter. My mind is at ease as we make plans. Rinchen will take us to Rumbak Valley, within the Hemis National Park, next morning. Only part of the route can be covered by vehicle, the last 3,000 feet must be tackled by foot. I think it wise not to inform Rinchen that my fear of heights borders on vertigo. As it is, I am deeply embarrassed by the paucity of preparations. Rinchen rattles out the bare necessities: thermals, sweaters, insulated jackets, glares, chocolates and other such quick energisers. Woefully unprepared, Alwin and I beg, borrow and steal. We finally start early the next morning, driving by the River Indus before the mountains take over. The landscape is harsh and incredible, a vast expanse of dull desert bordered by mountains painted in different colours: white, mud brown, chocolate, dull maroon tinted with a hint of orange. We drive over rickety bridges, around hairpin bends and on roads so narrow I wonder how the jeep fits in them. The road ends at Zinchen, a tiny cluster of houses with more dogs than people.

We stop to rest. Alwin is in his own paradise, surrounded by umpteen photo opportunities. I wander around followed by canine faithfuls, lured by a packet of biscuits I am generous with.

All the terraces in the villages sport a strange contraption: mirrors propped by a pair of bharal horns. Bharals are a favourite snow leopard meal and are called Blue Sheep, even if they are neither blue nor sheep, but a sort of feral goat. To get back to the point, the 'horn mirror' is a source of solar electricity. Here in this remote corner on the roof of India the sun continues to provide warmth through bitterly cold nights.

Seeing strangers, the villagers gather around us, exchange pleasantries and inform us that the *shen* had recently visited the village to hunt livestock penned in rather flimsy wooden barriers. The animal is a vampire, vouch the villagers, sucking the blood of its victims, rarely eating the flesh.

This belief stems from the fact that the leopard kills by suffocating the jugular vein as life and blood ebbs out. Usually it slinks away with just one animal, but the trauma of a leopard in their midst is fatal for the rest of the livestock.

The villagers do not take kindly to such nocturnal visits, but admit there are benefits. The *shen* is their butcher. Being Buddhists, they do not kill for their supper, so the big cat does their job, especially in the harsh winters.

There is this story of a little girl who kept picking up goats even as the leopard was killing them. She kept screaming, terrified by the leopard but unwilling to desert such an unexpected treat. As each goat disappeared into the girl's basket, the leopard killed

The KING and I

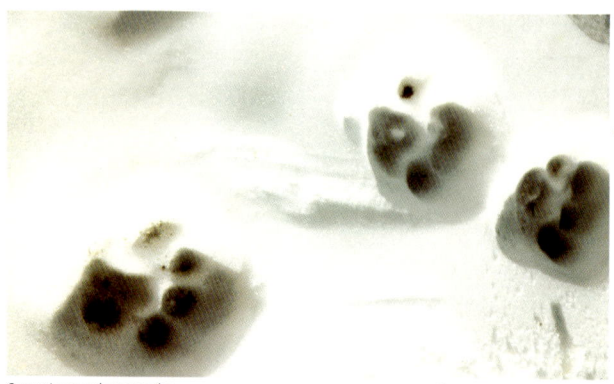

Snow Leopard pugmarks

For epochs to come the peaks will still pierce the lonely vistas, but when the last Snow Leopard has stalked amongst the crags, a spark of life will be gone turning the mountains into stones of silence

George Schaller, 1977

River Indus

another to assuage his hunger. So excited was the girl by this unexpected bounty that she did not realise that the leopard still had its fangs in the goat she was stuffing in her basket. The leopard won the tug of war and slunk away to enjoy his meal, leaving the girl to feast on hers.

Rinchen tells me that in rare cases, villagers have avenged the loss of livestock. The cat seldom strikes back, strangely submissive as it is herded into a corner by an angry mob, which stones the animal to death. There is no recorded history of a man-eater snow leopard, unlike the leopard of the plains.

Leopard lore at its best, it goads me on, providing the much-needed adrenaline to climb the additional 2,200 feet to Rumbak. I walk on ice, amid cliffs dressed in snow, with Rinchen leading the way. He is a child of the mountains, nimbly tackling

Snow Leopard

the tough climb as I lumber behind. Rinchen kindly refers to my clumsy attempts as *Sumsak*, the local dance not known for its grace.

I turn at a bend, coming face to face with a monstrous, hairy animal, the *dzo*, a cross between the yak and the domestic cow. It gives me a brooding look, which does little for my confidence. Size matters and I am at a distinct disadvantage. Choices, choices. The beast ahead and a sheer fall below. I take my chances with the animal and am rewarded for my trust. I squeeze past, unhurt.

I witness the snow leopard, in parts. The first find is the scat, in other words snow leopard excreta. And before you screw your nose in disgust, this is the key to the mystery cat; giving all sorts of important information like the food it eats, how long ago it ate, its health. I smell a rock next, where the big cat has spayed. In cat language this is advertisement for potential mates, and a warning to contesting males. It tells us that the leopard was here less than a day ago. There are pugmarks on the road, and while not conclusive, Rinchen suspects they belong to an old friend. A young male he has been monitoring through remote sensor cameras. I follow the pugmarks reverently with the eerie feeling that I am walking his walk. Finally, on the trail! But it is not to be; the pugmarks disappear, phantomlike, like the animal we pursue. The predator proves elusive, but his prey is aplenty, herds of bharal sauntering over precarious cliffs as though walking on the national highway. We see an unidentified lizard poised over a rock and the Lammergeyer soaring in the sky above.

Five miles and 3,000 feet later, we are in Rumbak, sipping *gud gud chai*, tea brewed with milk, salt and yak butter. For lunch there is *skew*, the Ladakhi version of pasta prepared with wheat balls served in herbal sauce. Rumbak is a hamlet of just nine households. The clock

Author with Rinchen at Rumbak Valley

151

The KING and I

Bharal or Blue Sheep

winds back a hundred years here – old men weave shawls, women milk the tethered *dzos* and the bathroom is an outhouse with the throne, just a hole perched at a considerable height. Rinchen departs, leaving us to the tender mercies of Padma. Her home is humble but the rustic comforts beat the luxuries of a five star hotel.

Dinner is by the fire, spiced with tales of the big cat. They are neighbours, the people of the valley and the predator, an unwelcome guest for the occasional meal. Even so not one person here has seen the leopard.

I cuddle into my blanket at night, tossing restlessly, unable to sleep. I am here, at last, in the snow leopard's sanctuary. So near, and yet so far, I muse before drifting off to sleep. I am jerked awake by a mew precariously close to the door. I remember my lessons of the day;

this big cat does not roar, it mews. I strain my ears but fail to catch any sound. Foolishly, I step out. It is pitch dark, the silence frightening. Hurriedly, I step back into the safety of the room and move to latch the door. I spot it then, a mere flash of silver gray disappearing into the night. I pinch myself, I am awake. And I have seen, actually seen the snow leopard. Or at least its tail, arguably the most attractive feature of the animal. The tail is as long as the leopard's body and is used to balance in the tough terrain. It's thick and woolly and the leopard curls it around its body for warmth. Later, in the morning, I hear more tail tales. Mama leopard throws it over cliffs to help her young climb. It serves as a disciplinarian tool as well; she makes a huge noise by smashing it on the ground as a warning to erring cubs.

I sleep in peace. I have seen the snow leopard. Not a soul believes me, though. I'm told that I was dreaming, sleepwalking, I spin a fantastic yarn, that the fancy leopard sighting is a figment of my feverish imagination. I don't care. I am walking on clouds.

We get a sample of village life, women toiling in fields (13,000 feet above sea level, it boggles the mind), weaving cane baskets and *durries*. We take a walk, sharing the route with yet more bharal. Lunch is *chappatis* made with freshly ground wheat and butter churned from *dzo* milk. Repast over; it is time to make our way back to Zinchen, where the vehicle awaits us. By now we are old hands on this icy path. If you discount minor mishaps like a sprained ankle and falling flat on ice-cold water.

On the flight back, I peer down at the snow-clad mountains below; I am informed we go right over Rumbak Valley. I imagine that somewhere in the vast icy world below is my Phantom of the Mountains.

Tigers of the Emerald Forests

Panna is beautiful tiger country, with the River Ken meandering across its three plateaus. My main motivation for going to Panna, besides my irrepressible wildlife addiction, was the ongoing telemetric tiger study in the park, which had unravelled some lesser-known facets of this mysterious cat.

Diamonds are harvested in this tigerland. Panna is home to the oldest diamond mines of the country, and while commerce and nature have co-existed for years, the ravages of the former have left a cancerous scar in these emerald forests. How magnificent these forests must have been once, burgeoning with game. 'The horizon seemed covered with forests, not scanty, but virgin forests, abounding with peafowl. A herd of sambhar issued forth, advanced toward us at full speed, making the ground tremble between them', wrote French traveller Louis Rousselet while on a tiger hunt in 'Punnah' in the eighteenth century. I was on a tiger hunt too, but of a different kind.

Think tiger. And the mind and the heart conjures up images of power, strength, mystery, grace, stealth, danger and awesome beauty. Simply put, the tiger is the most charismatic species on earth. Certainly, it has commanded the maximum attention. An exclusive project has been devoted to its conservation, coupled with immense international support. It remains the focus of media attention, and I would reckon there are more books on the tiger, than tigers in the wild. Even confirmed non-naturalists are not unaffected by the plight of the tiger. But despite this overwhelming interest, little is known about the tiger. Agreed, it is the air of mystery that makes the creature so special. The tiger is an enigma. I have met the cat several times in Indian forests and even the briefest of encounters has become a cherished moment. But each meeting, while deeply satisfying, is equally frustrating.

I long to know more about the predator, even the simplest basics. How much does a tiger eat? What is the territory it must command to get its regular meal supply? Are the needs of the male and the female the same? The answers are mostly guesswork. There are few studies, and those desirous to know the science of wild tigers must still turn to George Schaller's *The Deer and Tiger*, published in 1967.

The KING and I

The tigers of the emerald forests of Panna are as elusive, as mysterious. But ever so slowly the mist is clearing, allowing a privileged glimpse into the secret life of the tiger. *Panna ka pattawala sherni ki maut*, it was this story in a local newspaper on the poaching of one of the radio-collared tigers of Panna which led me to Dr. Raghu Chundawat, the tall, soft-spoken scientist who had been leading a telemetric study on Panna tigers for the past eight years. The study aimed to understand and assess ecological requirements to maintain a viable tiger population.

The signals emanating from the collar are picked up by handheld directional antennae, which help in locating the tiger and indicate its behaviour and activity. This, coupled with other studies, helps in understanding their survival needs and such data is utilised for their conservation. This is the first study of its kind in dry, tropical forests, which is typical of most tiger habitat in India. Tigers are most vulnerable in such habitats since density of prey is low and water, scarce. Raghu explains some findings, I am not too good with science, but essentially I understand that the tigers of Panna have a large home range, at times the males may cover thirty-five kilometres in a day, implying they are constantly on the move. Females tend to roam less, they stay close to the cubs. Finding receptive females marks a tiger's territory, while it is the intensity of prey base that decides the tigress' nursery. To put it more crudely, the male wants sex, while the woman wants food for the family. I am some years too late to witness the tiger being collared but I am sure that it is no cakewalk to tranquillise this massive beast and fit it with a collar. It's risky, both for the human and the tiger. The test to check if the chemical has taken effect, and the predator dead to the world, is to pull the tiger by its tail. Raghu remembers the feeling of awe and terror when he held the mighty beast's head beneath his sweating palms.

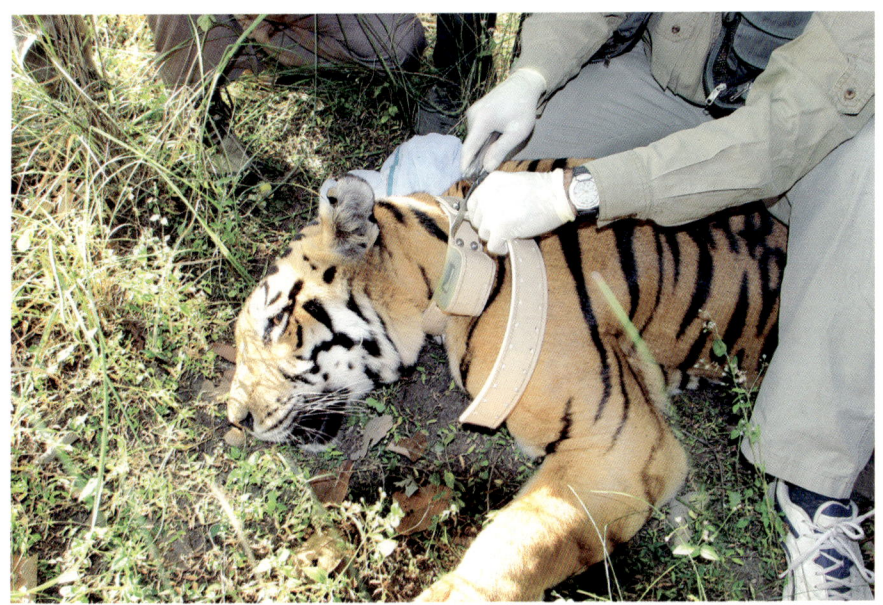

All this tiger talk propelled me to plan a trip to this forest neighbouring India's erotic capital Khajuraho. Though Panna is in India's tiger state, Madhya Pradesh, it has not featured with prominence on India's tourist map. Not a surprise, considering that most of the visitors concentrate on Khajuraho temples…sex sells! Panna is usually an afterthought.

I arrive at the forest resthouse too late for a safari but the night is not futile, as I listen, with enthusiasm, to yet more tales about the collared tigers of Panna, this time from forests guards and trackers who spend their days and nights, patrolling the jungle.

No two tigers are alike. It is not just the stripes that mark their individuality. Each tiger has its own peculiar character and behaviour. Most tigers in Panna are identified by their radio frequency number, except Ms 52, who has earned her sobriquet by her eyebrow markings, which read like the numbers five and two. She is, literally, the mother of all tigers. Her family tree now spreads to over thirty cubs, well into their fourth generation. She is getting on in years but age has not dimmed her ferocity. Her exploits around these parts are legendary and one can safely conclude that this tiger is certainly not Miss Congeniality. She has a reputation of not taking things lying down. Nor does she take kindly to humans or elephants. Mohanlal, a forest guard, remembers, with unrestrained glee, the plight of a tourist who almost fell on top of her in fright, when she charged the elephant he was on. On another occasion she decided to take on a jeep, placing her heavy paw on the bonnet. The jeep inched backwards and she forward, her face just a whisker away from the driver. Snarling, roaring with rage, she made her intent clear: that collar or not, she was the Boss. King, or in her case, Queen of the forest. For all her belligerence, Ms 52 has never hurt

The KING and I

Scent-marking territory

anyone, backing off after she has delivered a good scare. Such behavior arouses my curiosity, it is not the first time I have witnessed it. Charger owed his name to his aggressive behaviour, though never seriously enough to hurt anyone. Boxer at Sariska had displayed similar behaviour. What was it that motivated such mock charges? Was it anger, frustration at being constantly disturbed, or, just a wicked sense of fun?

Another collared tiger is 125, now past his prime. In his day, he has done his job of perpetuating his line rather well, spreading his genes by mating with 52, 120 and 113 and a few others not blessed by name or number.

Ms 120 is a particularly tragic story. Unlike her mother, Ms 52, she was the genial sort and was not much bothered by the human race or the presence of elephants. She did not value privacy and loved being out in the open giving both scientists, and tourists, a peek into her life. But not for long. 120 was killed on the fringes of Panna, walking into a trap while she was hunting for food for her cubs. She died slowly and painfully, well before her time, ensnared in a poacher's noose, life slowly oozing out of her. Her life, and indeed death, left many questions unanswered. It highlighted the vulnerability of tigers and the urgency to protect them. Raghu is mystified by the fact that she taught her cubs to kill and hunt, to climb trees when they were very young, perhaps too young. Did she have a premonition about her death? Did she want to teach them as much as she could before she left? Science has no answers.

I grieve for 120 and long to meet 52, though I am worried about her confrontational instincts. Why did 120 have to die? Where are her orphaned cubs now? With such troubled thought I drift into an uneasy slumber. My sleep is interrupted by an insistent *aaunnghh... aaunn .. aaunn..ungh*, the call of the tiger, a soft sound rolling over the jungle like a gentle wave, so unlike its full throated, terrifying roar. Who was it? Who knew? I like to think it is Mr 125, parading his domain and on the prowl for a prospective mate.

The next morning is unproductive, tiger-wise, but then Panna has so much more. The Ken, surely one of India's most spectacular rivers, flows through its forests, often silent and sometimes roaring down the gorges. If I missed the tiger, its prey is aplenty. Panna is virtually a supermarket, offering the King a succulent array of deer meat. Prey species are always on the alert for any untoward sight or sound. Most vanish at the sound of the jeep. The cheetal, apparently the braver sort, look stoically at the jeep and refuse to give way. The sambhar is his Majesty's most preferred meal for its bulk. Nilgai — or blue cow, a name that has afforded it much protection in a country where cows are sacred — is huge and ungainly and supremely indifferent to our presence. The four-horned antelope or the *chowsingha* is the most fidgety of the lot, bounding away at the slightest rustle. A foreign tourist used his broken Hindi to ask the guide how he distinguished between the sexes of the antelope. 'Male horny, female not,' replied the guide in his broken English. 'Ditto men,' said I.

The next two days are a blur. I scour the jungle for tigers without much luck. I sail down the River Ken, crossing evil-eyed crocodiles that watch me malevolently as if sizing their dinner. I have shifted base to Ken River Lodge, a languid jungle resort. The buzz is usually at the Bar, a beautifully constructed tree house in *Gular* trees. Vinni Singh, a passionate naturalist, with a special interest in small cats, owns the resort. If he is to be believed, Panna has the highest concentration of these and also boasts of the rare caracal.

Sketch of Tiger 123

The KING and I

Siesta has to be timed with the macaques since we share living space. Much before dawn, the roof thunders with the sound of langurs, bounding from tree to roof and back, screeching and hooting to their mates, and the world in general.

After lending an impatient ear to the langurs, I leave for the morning safari. This time, I meet the angels of death: hyenas scavenging on the remains of a kill while vultures encircle overhead, waiting for their turn to feast. It is a rare sight, for the vulture population has dropped by ninety per cent in recent years, but I yearn for Mr. and Mrs. Stripes. It is not to be. Panna's collared tigers choose to stay away, at least from me.

I hear from a little further away the warning signals of terrified simians, the tiger crossed my path behind the jeep, though I didn't realise it. By the time I swung my head backwards, it was gone. Of course, the jeep behind had a good look as it strolled in front of their vehicle. *Damn*. Later I learn that it was Miss 113, daughter of granny 52 and it was seen by most of the river lodge. Local lore proclaims that while Miss 113 has an even temperament most of the time, she has been known to lose her cool occasionally. She has mothered three litters and is now cavorting with an unidentified male. While others chatter away excitedly about their close encounter, I slink away, feeling like Cinderella missing her royal ball.

Will I see the tiger? I, and a virtual army of tiger trackers and guides have tried their best, following pugmarks, alarm calls and other such clues. They are around, but I do not see them. And so, irrationally, I turn to the supernatural. I visit the grave of Baba Badami with my offering of five coconuts. Baba Badami is a local legend around here. He was a hermit who spent many years in the forest, though few can pinpoint the exact time. He had some kind of power over tigers, almost like a magnetic pull. It is said that they would sit with the Baba for hours, in peace, as he meditated. They would come to him when ill and wounded.

Baba cured them. He just needed to think tigers, and they would appear as though obeying a silent command. Local hoteliers seek Baba Badami when a tiger is not sighted for days, I usually dismiss such stuff as utter nonsense, but here I surrender to the spell of the tiger. Baba, I pray as I break the coconuts…don't disappoint me.

It is my last day in Panna and I spend it atop an elephant, walking on uneven roads frequented by the feline predator. Still no tiger, collared or otherwise, crosses my cursed path. By this time, I feel I know the tigers of Panna. I have stayed up nights talking about them, poring over their pictures, learning about their quirks and idiosyncrasies. They seem like old friends, 52, 113, 125 & Co. But I will go back without meeting any of them. Or so I think. My moment of despair, and the peace of the jungle, is suddenly shaken by a massive, spine-chilling roar. The air reverberates with the savage sound, leaves vibrate involuntarily and a terrified animal kingdom responds in a cacophony of terror. Tiger!

My elephant, Anarkali, picks up maddening speed, following the jungle telegraph that leads me to the tigress and her freshly killed prey. I am close, so close I can hear her steady breath. See her burning gold through the green foliage that separates us. Admire her strength as her muscles ripple under her incredible coat. Respect her supremacy as I witness her deadly canines sink into lifeless flesh. Fear her wrath as I sense her golden-amber eyes watching me, assessing my every move.

It is a tense moment and I am clearly at a disadvantage. She doesn't move, not a muscle. Just her eyes narrow, her teeth pull back in an agitated snarl. The warning is unmistakable, I have interrupted her meal. I had better move away. Reluctantly, joyously, I concede, thrilled at this royal rendezvous.

Did Baba Badami have a hand in this encounter, I wonder? Common sense says no, it was just incredible luck. I came to Panna hoping to understand tigers better, but they – thankfully – remain as much of an enigma as ever. The more you know, you realise how little you actually do. My thirst for a deeper insight on tigers has if anything, deepened. I hear Kanha now has radio-collared tigers, and Sundarbans is next in the line. I make plans….

Four-horned Antelope

The Vicerine's Bounty

Kaziranga occupies an important place in the world wildlife map as the single important gene pool of the Greater One-horned Rhinoceros. It is also the only reserve where the presence of the tiger is overshadowed by the quantum of other big game — rhinos, elephants and wild buffaloes in 430 square kilometres forest asylum. As it happens, Kaziranga boasts the highest tiger density, averaging 16.8 tigers per 100 square kilometres, far above to the average of one to 12 in most reserves. Wildlife sighting is easy in Kaziranga, the vast grasslands reminiscent of the African savannah, and the park a rare success story. Kaziranga is emulated in all my fervent prayers to the Almighty, Please God, bless the other parks, may they flourish as Kaziranga!

Every time I visit a forest, I feel like a child taking its first step into a whole new world. I feel a sense of wonder, overwhelmed by the immense beauty that envelops me. But sorrow follows the thrill like a black shadow. An intense despair that deepens as one is confronted with the litany of problems that plague India's wilderness. Most of her parks are tragic tales of constant struggles, weariness is a faithful companion of the forest staff battling against poachers, developers, politicians and just about everyone out to exploit the wealth of the forest. Poachers sold all the tigers of Sariska, a tragedy echoed around the country. Graziers have colonised Ranthambhore, Gir and so many others. Militants have hijacked Nagarjunasagar and Indravati to name but a few, while pure lethargy and sense of defeat plagues Hazaribagh, and in my view most of India's parks.

The KING and I

Lord Curzon

In this overall gloomy picture, Kaziranga stands tall. She has her share of problems as all naturally wealthy must, but this is one park which stands out, as that rare conservation success story, resurrected from the rubble to become the last and only stronghold of the highly endangered Greater One-horned Rhinoceros.

I visited Kaziranga on its hundredth birthday and for one so ancient it must be said that she has aged well. Like good wine, the park has enriched with the passage of time.

Kaziranga has a colourful conservation history, and like Gir, the fortunes of this park turned with the intervention of Lord Curzon, or more accurately, his good wife Lady Victoria Curzon. She was ill-advised to visit it; no one could enter the place. It was a leech-infested swamp, which even elephants found difficult to circumvent. Heedless, she ventured in, motivated by an unmitigated desire to see the rare rhinoceros. Her visit was futile, for all she saw was a set of hooves imprinted in the soggy marshes. Worried about their impending doom, the Vicerine urged her husband to save this beleaguered creature. Consequently, in September 1905, the chief commander of Assam passed an order for the preservation of game in Kaziranga. There was to be no hunting, no human habitation and no cultivation within this preserve.

Since then, Kaziranga has seen many saviours. E. P. Gee, a tea planter, became the park's greatest advocate. Forest Officer Milroy curbed extensive poaching within the park as did Mahi Chandran Miri whose courage is legendary. Then there are hundreds of unsung heroes, nameless forest guards, who fiercely protect the rhino in the most abysmal of conditions. Kaziranga is a rare success story with just over 1,500 rhinos now, a significant jump from just a handful a century back.

After a perfunctory, hasty jaunt – though I did spot elephants and a few assorted herbivores — in the park, I joined the birthday party outside. It had been organised on a grand scale, with the park all trussed up to receive the exalted dignitaries. As all government festivities go, this one too was marked by chaos, and mired by controversies. Accommodation had been goofed up, invitations to important dinners and events arrived long after the episode was over. Activists riled against the commotion amidst the wilderness. I ignored the protests, otherwise perfect fodder for a journo, so elated was I at this rare cause to celebrate in conservation, though I must say that I was miffed at the 'Sexy Baby Pinky Musical Night' scheduled as part of the commemorations.

The elephant festival, part of the function, is significant because elephants are intrinsic to Indian religion and mythology. Arguably, the most beloved and endearing of India's Gods is the elephant-headed deity, Ganesha. The festival was an attempt to revive the ancient bond between man and beast ravaged by the bitter conflict brought on by man's encroachment into the elephant's habitat. This battle has no winners, elephants maraud people who come in their way, and humans, in turn, kill the elephants in revenge. One particular incident, just after 9/11, said it all. Eighteen elephants had been poisoned in and around Nameri National Park in a period of four months. One massive elephant, killed by enraged villagers lay lifeless in its own blood. Scrawled on the carcass was *Dhan Chor* (Osama) *Bin Laden*. Paddy thief Bin Laden. God had morphed into a thief and terrorist.

But here the mood, in contrast to such horror, was festive and upbeat. It was an elephantine congregation, about fifty of the mammoths adorned in rich red velvet tapering down to delicate anklets encircling each massive leg. They appeared unused to such formal attire, reminding me of wayward school children burgeoned and cajoled into marching in precise order to greet honourable guests. Largely they behaved impeccably, with some notable exceptions. Parboti rebelled against military discipline and charted her own route, halting at each tree to grab a tasty morsel. Ramu stopped short of a wooden bridge, which made him uncomfortable. He could see a pool of water below. Elephants' love for water is

The Greater One-horned Rhinoceros

The KING and I

Maharani Gayatri Devi with author Mark Shand at the festival

legendary and he followed his instincts by plunging into the puddle, squealing in delight at this unexpected treat. But it was Baby Rinky who stole the show. Oblivious of the grandeur and solemnity of the occasion, she sauntered along in whimsical abandon, stuffing biscuits, breads and bananas that an adoring public excitedly pushed her way. She came up to me, a diminutive pachyderm, barely a-year-old yet taller than me. She sniffed the air probingly, then her tiny trunk shot out, dipping delicately in my pocket to extract the lone sweet that nestled inside. Glee, then puzzlement reflected in her eyes and I could sense her wrestling with the problem of removing the wrapper that obstructed her feast. With great care, she placed the candy in my outstretched palm, an expectant look in her eye. I removed the offending plastic and in a moment the sweet was gone. As was Rinky, gambolling ahead joyfully, taking with her my heart and a solemn commitment to do well for her kind.

The wayward elephant convoy paraded on, watched by an indulgent crowd. All wanted rides, while a few sought the reassurance of touch. A young man, an ex-militant I later learnt,

The elephant festival

bowed his head at a passing elephant. An old woman, clutching a baby, bent in obeisance to touch the feet of another. "Bless my son, Ganesha…" Change does not happen overnight, it moves slowly but surely, rather like the animal in question. I do not imagine that old wounds will be wiped off in a day by this elephantine cavalcade but the healing process now had a chance. Looking at the pompous parade, still holding its audience spellbound, the links fell into place. I thought of the wild elephants I had observed that morning inside Kaziranga. Just like humans, elephants too form a tightly knit family group, and I could see one such. Mothers, babies and aunts, bathing and cavorting in the mighty Brahmaputra River. They stepped out, impossibly silent for their size, the matriarch in front and another holding guard at the rear, with the babies herded in between for safety. Slowly they melted into the grass. A small representation of the 25,000 odd elephants that exist today in India's wilds.

I remembered the bitterness of a farmer I met a few days back, a man who had lost his entire crop, and a brother, to the hunger and rage of a displaced wild herd. His eyes were bloodshot with barely unshed tears and bewilderment: Why were the Gods angry? But he too knew that the Gods were distressed; pressed for space and starved for food.

Rinky and her ilk are the best bet to bridge this gap. They are the ambassadors of their kind, tamed elephants living with man, gently teaching him their ways, captivating the audience so that their wild cousins can continue to live and flourish.

Dawn was still to arrive when I entered the precincts of the park the next day, my early start an attempt to escape the madding crowds that had collected for the celebrations. As the skies brightened, a delicate mist wisped through the grass, dewdrops glistened and the

Local girls pause for rest

cacophony of a multitude of unidentified birds filled the air. Daybreak at Kaziranga is a spectacular transition from drab grey to brilliant gold.

I was luckier than Lady Edwina, spotting a rhino within minutes of entering the park. It was a huge lumbering creature with drooping skin, mean disposition, a mass of ungainly hair protruding on its head and an unsteady gait. It peered at us, lips curled in a sneer, and was so impossibly ugly a creature that he looks ruggedly handsome. Imagine surviving unchanged for twenty-five million years. Its armour plate is said to be a gift from Lord Krishna, and *Rhinoceros unicornis* is the origin of the legend of the unicorn.

I was suitably impressed and its ugly contours took on an attractive shape. It was a cursed species, though, persecuted for its horn or the glued mass of hair wrongly attributed with aphrodisiacal and other wondrous qualities. It is much sought after by hunters for the huge price it commands amongst the rich, ignorant impotents of the world. The survival of the rhino is yet another miracle of Kaziranga, this creature has been hunted long before the lion and the tiger became prized trophies. Rhinos existed during the Mohenjodaro era about 5,000 years ago in the plains of the Indus; Emperor Babar described in his memoirs his rhino hunt in the Indus Valley in 1519. Intensive hunting and loss of habitat almost made the rhino extinct till the intervention of the benevolent Lady Curzon.

It is hard to believe that the rhino is an endangered creature. Here in the park there is a surfeit of them, lurking at every nook and corner of the landscape. I saw several, including one precariously positioned over a female for the purpose of procreation. I couldn't see the poor lady's face as she bore his bulk, but the male had a curiously bland, almost bored, expression for one engaged in such a task. With a final heave, he detached himself, sauntering off without a glance at the future mother of his children. Men are the same across all species!

What is special about Kaziranga is the pageant of wildlife on offer. It's like a theatre, you sit back and watch the denizens parade by. Each animal is a character, playing his part in the larger drama of life. It may not reveal all its secrets, and the script and characters will change according to the mood and season. This unpredictability within the promise of a grand show is what I loved about Kaziranga.

The rhinos had done their part. The elephants, both wild and domestic had dominated the preceding day. I took a privileged seat and stationed myself on the edge of a waterbody in the eastern range of the park. I

Hog Deer

could see over a dozen rhinos munching uncaringly, while wild buffaloes, with their wide horns narrowing menacingly, did much the same. Lunchtime, I presume. A hog deer sauntered by, initially indifferent then lifting its delicate nose to sniff the air. It came closer, its doe like eyes outlined with curling eyelashes I could die for. I sat stock-still and so close was it that I could feel the heat of its body. The moment was shattered by the sudden snort of the buffalo whose peace had been disturbed by a wild boar, who had dared to get too close. The bovine upturned its nose, throwing and tossing its huge head back and forth. Its horns slashed the air like rapiers and I was well reminded that this was not the placid buffalo of rural India, milked by cowherds and bullied by young kids. The horns of the wild buffalo are deadly weapons and only the rhino surpasses the unpredictability of this animal. But after a little tantrum and generally establishing its superiority, the bovine got down to serious business of chewing the cud.

I could see an occasional egret nitpicking and hopping from one herbivore to another. A huge black bird with a protruding, almost vulgar pouch stood defiantly in the foreground. If looks are discounted, then this was a prize sight, for there live only 150 of the Greater Adjutant Stork in India.

Silk Cotton or the Semul trees, their red flowers setting the forest on fire, framed the water. Pelicans roosted on them, their huge lower beak appearing larger than the bird itself. An inane Ogden Nash limerick came instantly to mind: A strange bird is the pelican, whose beak holds more than its belly can. That such a place, where God's creatures roam free and

The KING and I

Asiatic Wild Buffalo

safe is nothing short of a miracle. Unwillingly, I hoisted myself to shift to another range, Baguri on the western side of the park. It was a well-timed departure, enroute in the River Diphu, the silt-ridden arm of the Brahmaputra, I had my first ever sighting of the Smooth-coated Otter. It was but a fleeting glimpse, three catlike, shimmery creatures gliding on their hindlegs, minding their own business when interrupted, I fancy, by the unpleasant scent of humans. In seconds they disappeared into the water, though one curious character bobbed up, as if to check if the intruders had gone. Disappointed to find us still standing there, it vanished under a ripple of bubbles, not to be seen again.

Just a morning in Kaziranga, yet so enriched with wildlife. The only big game I missed was the tiger. I like to keep up appearances that I am in the forest for the whole experience and not just the tiger. True, but not strictly so. Here, though, the big cat did not dwell on my mind nor was there even the faintest sense of loss at not sighting the predator. Kaziranga with its myriad denizens kept me enthralled.

The Gypsy passed by many a forest *chowki*, I stopped at one, chatted with the guards, who were equally game for some gossip. Life in the jungle can be lonely. Their huts, fashioned from bamboo are perched on stilts, and parked underneath is a dinghy. Mukund Bora, a guard explained to me that the boat is a crucial vehicle used to patrol the park, and even more so in times of flood, an annual ritual when most of the park is submerged in water. The life giving Brahmaputra turns into a hungry demon, devastating the land, swallowing the animals. Bora remembers that in the floods of 1998, forty rhinos lost their lives, and yet another guard lost his foot to a panicked rhino he tried to save. Poaching is another severe problem. In certain years hunters have ambushed nearly a hundred rhinos in the park. But the tide is slowly turning, and poaching in the park is almost down to nil in the past three years, thanks to the incessant patrolling by foresters and their relentless courage.

Our conversation was interrupted by the muted whirr of a bicycle. It was a forest guard on patrol. An almost defunct .315 rifle slung over his shoulder. I stopped him and exchanged notes. I gushed about the wonders I had witnessed that day. He smiled and extended his hand. Mutilated, I noticed. He shrugged when I asked the cause of the injury. A straying tiger had recently ravaged it. It was a mother with two cubs, and she had wandered into a village, causing panic and terror. He was part of the rescue team, to lead the tiger back to the park. It wasn't easy, a huge mob had gathered and the frightened tigress had struck, fearing for the safety of her cubs. "She was a mother, who could blame her?" he reasoned. He has had two encounters with poachers, too. In the first, they lost a few men, but in the latter the foresters came out unscathed, even though the poachers had more sophisticated weaponry. Doesn't he fear for his life, I ask. He shrugged, embarrassed. It's his work, it's the rhino and Kaziranga. All must be saved. He moves on, leaving us the gift of wild Kaziranga. Now I know the secret of its survival, a hundred years on.

Forest guard at Kaziranga

Armchair Naturalist

In 1965 conservationist E. R. C. Davidar set up Cheetal Walk *in the Sigur Forest at the foot of the Nilgiri hills. Beyond the verandah, the jungle stretched to the mountains, while in the west it wandered into Kerala. In its backyard, the forest extended into the four wildlife refuges of Mudumalai, Bandipur, Nagarhole and Wayanad.* Cheetal Walk *was a home in the heart of the wild. This was an experience far removed from my other forays in the forest. Everywhere else, I ventured into forests to seek the tranquillity of nature, for the thrill of sighting big game. Here, the peace and the drama of the wild came calling at my doorstep.*

'Rum! Get me two bottles of rum!' said a frantic voice at the other end of the line. I slam the phone down in a fluster. What am I letting myself into, I ask myself. Getting through to Cheetal Walk hadn't been easy; phones and such technological marvels are erratic in wilderness. It is only now, when I am practically at the doorstep that the call had finally come through. I had called to book a room, but the only response I get is a frenetic request for spirits. I arrive at Cheetal Walk, or Jungle Trails, the fancier name it has now acquired, with some trepidation, and lots of expectation. The latter I owe to the book *Cheetal Walk*, the story of Reggie Davidar's house nestling under the Nilgiris. This was a place where you didn't have to seek wildlife, wild animals sought you, instead.

I had been advised to carry with me Maggi-two-minute noodles and other such instant goodies. The cook, Sukumar, is known to disappear for indeterminate periods, and when around may be found in a drunken stupor and Mark Davidar, the current incumbent often forgot to eat. He works hard at being a genial host, but it's a monumental struggle. Mark is a character. Eccentric, endearing, comfortable with animals, averse to people.

Cheetal Walk is the sort of home I dream about. A comfortable, if rustic, cottage in the foothills, amidst the forest, neighbouring a stream, a well in the backyard and with a variety of wild denizens calling at the door. The welcome I get is a trifle tepid, since I do not possess either feathers or fur. Wildlife is the VIP here, humble humans eyed with a certain suspicion. Scripted on a fading, yellowing sheet of paper is a list of rules: Musical instruments, radios and tape-recorders are taboo, as are bright lights. No music, no loud noises, no walking around in the dark. 'I am going to add one more: Trespassers will be prostituted,' proclaims Mark. My steps falter, but Mike guffaws at his joke, ushers me inside his home – hotel or resort is too fancy a word – takes me to my room and offers a glass of rum which I politely refuse, considering that the sun has just woken up. My room, basic but cozy, has an

Left: Sloth Bear; above: Cheetal Walk

The KING and I

Ronaldo and Rivaldo

illustrious history, the legendary birdman Salim Ali is just one among many famous guests who camped here. Lock the door, warns Mark, it is a favourite haunt of wild animals, as well. There was this absentminded guest who forgot to latch the door, and hyenas walked in. Bears like the room, too, apparently. Mark once walked in on a sleeping bear, who had curled himself in a snug corner. Surely Mark was exaggerating? What had I let myself in for? I wondered again.

But then, wasn't this exactly why I was here? I had read *Cheetal Walk* with avid interest. Its untamed menagerie were old friends I longed to meet. Bumpty was an unusually good sort. He was an inquisitive, friendly elephant, who doubled up as a counsellor for Mark's brother in times of trouble. Then there was Udayar, the fun-loving bully who occasionally played with buffaloes, not to mention the tusker who politely rubbed his feet on the doormat before stepping into the verandah. This is good elephant country, and offered a great opportunity to understand these animals. Mark says they are not unlike men, but, of course, they are much better. To quote from the book, 'they can be affable or crusty, noisy or quiet, aggressive or amiable, they displayed a whole range of human behavioural patterns, except they are less complicated'.

Other than the assorted pachyderms, there was Adam the Bear, who liked to tell the world when he copulated; the cunning, wild dogs who whistled and brayed in frightening concert and the hyena who came for his bag of bones...

I was in for a rude shock. Reality had reared its ugly head even in this secluded haven. The tuskers of old are no more: most butchered by poachers for their ivory, a threat that has

Nilgiri Foothills

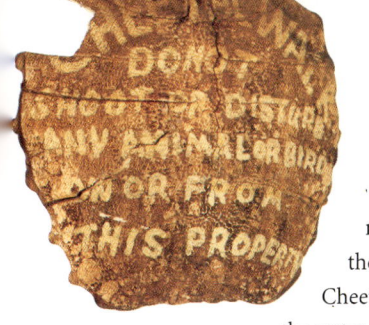

become acute in the past few years. Elephants are sacred, but even Gods are butchered when they yield money. I ache to think that the tuskers, brought to life in the book, were now dead. Wild elephants still frequent Cheetal Walk more so than before. It is not just the stream or the water tank built by the Davidar family, or even the salt lick – crucial to beasts for their quota of calcium – that draws them. Perhaps, they feel safe, here, in Cheetal Walk, among friends who will not harm, even as sanctuaries fail to provide succour.

The new lot of elephantine visitors is a football team, most have been christened after football players, the game being Mark's only abiding interest outside of animals. Kafu is the biggest and bulkiest of the lot, and thus bears the Brazilian captain's name. Ronaldo, like his namesake, is a tornado, wreaking havoc on drums, plants and anything that comes in his way. His bosom pal Rivaldo, another tusker, knows what he wants – whether it be a drink of water or the ambrosia he can spy in the cook's hut – but achieves it in a subtle, cunning manner, minus the brash bravado of Ronaldo. They are regular visitors, usually dropping by in the evenings. Just sit in the verandah, advises Mark, and let the show begin. Animal Planet, live, for the slouch potato.

It's a bit hard to take in. Big game usually plays shy, veiled with the protective cover of the forest. It requires much patience, diligent effort and some luck for a forest to yield game. I have lost count of the number of times I have been on the prowl in sanctuaries, on foot, in jeeps, on boats, astride an elephant and camel-back. Always alert, forever hopeful for any

creature of the wild. At Cheetal Walk, life is simpler and the boot is on the other foot, so to speak. Park yourself on the front verandah, armed with camera, binoculars and beer, if so inclined. But be warned, elephants love alcohol, and nothing – but nothing – comes in the way of the beast and his drink.

Mark settles himself in his favourite chair and has warned me off it. It is for his exclusive use. Wildlife exempted, of course. On several occasions leopards curl up on this chair at night, leaving strands of hair on the cushion as a memento. More comfortable, I imagine, than freezing atop a tree on a cold night.

I burrow into an armchair and delve into a bowl of chips provided by Sukumar, who has admirably refrained from drink. The Maggi, fortunately, may lie untouched. Sukumar is a story in himself, he belongs to the ancient Kurmba tribe, originally bought as slaves from the north by the Mughals to catch and tame wild elephants. Today, the government employs their descendants as mahouts, but their skills are dying. Mahouts are not much in demand now, and the younger generation has shifted to more lucrative opportunities in cities. I can see a herd of cheetal, walking with their usual grace, a blur of white spots in a sea of brown. A wild boar pushes its nose inquisitively on the front step before deciding that our company is not to his liking. The landscape is breathtaking. Cheetal Walk is on a plinth overlooking a stream and the Nilgiris beyond. The evening is serene, the silence often punctuated by the disoriented cry of a peacock. A strikingly beautiful bird with a decidedly bad throat. Vain in his beauty, God must have thought it best not to gift him with a melodious voice as well!

The Football Team has failed to show up. Unfair, I grumble, feeling cheated. Just as I am to give up for the day, a bear walks upstream. It's a Mama Bear, with cub riding piggyback. After a cool drink, the sloth bear dislodges a stone, digs the soft earth to extract termites

Left: Striped Hyena; below: Monkey Puss, the pet Palm Civet; right: Giant Squirrel

or other such delicious morsels. Bears are unpredictable creatures, more of a risk than a tiger would be in the wild.

Post-dinner, Mark leaves for some serious work, a drink with his pals, but not before issuing strict instructions to lock doors and not to walk in the dark if I want to steer clear of elephants, bears and other wild animals. Cut it out, Mark, as if I would. A city slicker like me is already having a hard enough time getting used to the eerie stillness. The next second, I desperately wish for the silence as a wild, maniacal laughter shrieks through the night. My brain freezes; my heart misses a thousand beats. Is it a ghost? A lunatic? No, it's a hyena, my numbed brain registers. A braver heart than mine would have rejoiced, a hyena in the wild is an increasingly rare sight and a pack so close is one for the record. I try convincing myself that I am indeed fortunate. This isn't easy. The little knowledge that I have scraped together says that hyenas are scavengers and feed on the dead. It isn't a pleasant thought; sleep is an erratic visitor that night.

Daybreak and a hot bath later, I am up on a *machan*, a crude platform on a tree near the stream, for a bird's eyeview on the wildlife that converges to quest their thirst beneath. It is an uneventful morning with 'only' the peacocks

The KING and I

Crested Serpent Eagle

Changeable Hawk Eagle

and cheetal dropping by. Only? I feel a little ashamed of my greedy mind, never satisfied, always wanting more and plagued with the unflagging desire to see the tiger.

Post-lunch, I park myself on the verandah to maintain my armchair vigil. There is some excitement in the backyard, a giant squirrel has fallen down the well. Sukumar plays hero, a futile effort, as it happens. He careens down the well, and comes up with a lifeless squirrel. It had not survived the fall. This event sets Mark in a melancholy mood, reminiscing about animals loved and lost. He rambles on about elephants, pointing to a tree where he had hung a tyre. Originally for visiting kids, but as it turned out the pachyderms loved it better. They were irrepressibly attracted to the suspended tyre; they played with it, tore it or carried it back home. Finding discarded tyres became quite tiresome, and finally, Mark gave up. Mostly he talks about his pet palm civet Monkey Puss, also called Sant Longowal, as its bushy tail resembled the slain Sikh saint's flowing beard! Orphaned as a kitten, she was adopted by the Davidar family. She had fallen from her nest hole and nurtured by Mark. She raised her litter in the washbasin of a room upstairs and was an aggressive mother. And like a true Cheetal

Walk denizen, she loved a bit of rum! Then one day, she left for the jungle, never to come back. Mark is a reluctant host, worried that the guest will disturb the tranquillity of the environs and interfere with the wild. Once this fear is dispelled, he becomes solicitous, enquiring about your food and well-being.

As dusk sets in, the mood mellows. In contrast, the jungle gets busy. Cheetal furiously mince grass, Mama bear puts in an appearance again, cub in tow and sambhars stroll by. The peace does not last long, peacocks shriek, monkeys whoop and the sambhar perks its ears and sprints for cover. Followed by a deathly silence, save for a sharp, short cry of agony. A predator has made a successful hunt. Much later, we go and investigate. Huge, squarish pugmarks tell that it was a male tiger. I can also see the tracks of the unfortunate victim. It was easy to tell where the tiger had sprung into action and the cow broken into a frenetic run. However cows are not conditioned to flee from tigers, and she must have been easy meat. The paucity of blood indicated a clean kill. Drag marks led into the thick undergrowth. The tiger had dragged its dinner to a more comfortable site. Meanwhile, with the immediate danger passing, the jungle calms down.

Peacocks resume their raucous call, the wind whistles, the sambhar emerges for a drink, and in the distance elephants trumpet. The Football Team, however, is ever elusive though Mark informs me later that no sooner had my car turned the corner, they marched by.

At night I manage a peaceful sleep, broken only by the hyenas' maniacal laughter. This time there are no missed heartbeats, no terror, only an abiding sorrow that I must leave Cheetal Walk, refuge of people and animals.

Wild Dog

The Big Game Show

Bandhavgarh, in Madhya Pradesh, is rich in tigers and their lore. It was the royal hunting ground for the Maharajas of Rewa, who aimed to shoot no less than 109 tigers, since this was considered an auspicious number that brought prosperity to the state. White tigers are also an 'endowment' of these forests; the genes of all captive white tigers in the world can be traced to Mohan, a wild cub caught and used as a stud by a Maharajah. Today, Bandhavgarh is perhaps the easiest place to see the Royal Bengal Tiger in the wild, pulling in an unprecedented number of cat maniacs. The result is mayhem.

The KING and I

I am caught in a traffic jam, somewhere in the middle of a convoy of thirty odd jeeps, and growing. New arrivals thunder in at regular intervals and screech to a halt. Guides uniformly dressed in camouflage green race frantically to an officious-looking man, wearily handing out tickets for Sher Darshan Programme, Bandhavgarh Bagh Yojana. Each such transaction is accompanied by intense squabbling and heated arguments. 'It's my turn!' shouts a florid foreigner, his voice drowned by a volley of unprintable Punjabi curses. The cacophony of *Homo sapiens* smothers the sounds and tranquillity of the jungle.

It is a luminous morning, mist and intense sun take turns to envelop and brighten the tall Sal trees. A leaf floats down, leisurely, like a broken kite fluttering to the earth below. A Junglefowl, a gaudier version of its domestic cousin, scurries by, while a pair of rare Red-headed Vultures peer down at us.

Not one person, among the hundred or so gathered, has an eye for the beauty that surrounds us. Not one ear is attuned to the rhythm of the forest. Each tourist here is waiting to see the tiger. All else is secondary, nothing else matters. The entire forest crew of Bandhavgarh is geared to show the pride of their jungle to the tourists. Each morning at five, mahouts and their elephants get to work, scouring the forest for signs of the tiger. Once it is located, elephants hem in the big cat to ensure it remains there. Walky-talkies buzz with the news. Word spreads fast: The tiger has been located, and 'pinned' down. Those who have booked themselves in advance for the show trundle over happily for the prized sighting. Those who had reluctantly opted out curse their misfortune and make their way to the theatre, nonetheless. They beg, they plead and then demand to see the tiger. The 'ticketman' assumes an air of importance, sometimes pompously acceding, at other times shrugging with

'White Tiger'

The Great Tiger Show

helplessness. With clockwork precision, two elephants — a magnificent male tusker and a daintier cow — carry a batch of four tourists, and ten minutes later park themselves next to a Gypsy, impatiently waiting for their load to disembark and another lot to clamber up. And so it goes on, till the entire lot have seen the tiger on show. Money exchanges hands, the mahouts are tipped handsomely. So hefty are the tips, it is said, that the mahout piles up a bigger sum than the wage of the park director!

I watch the proceedings with growing horror. This is my first 'tiger show'. The mist has given way to a harsh sun, and the squabbling is incessant. I tune myself out, my mind wanders to my previous 'tigerine' encounters; the sheer thrill of a tiger crossing my path while driving along forest roads or tracking pugmarks in the heart of the forest sitting atop an elephant. The thrill was in the surprise, at the rare unexpected encounter. 'Number 57,' someone yells urgently. That's my call. It's my turn, and I am reluctant to take it. I want to run away, away from this ridiculous circus that seeing the tiger has been reduced to. Of course, I want to see the tiger, I love the creature above all else, and each encounter fills me with an indescribable joy. But not like this, never like this. Too late to back out now, and I am pulled up onto the elephant by Ramzan, the mahout, to join the next set of tiger tourists. Ten minutes, warns the Ticketman, and off we go.

I find elephants endearing, in my book they are the best mode of jungle transport. The one that lumbers below me is particularly handsome. He is Indrajeet. Two huge, gleaming tusks protrude from under his cheeks. Deadly weapons, these tusks. Just the week before he had gored an aging matriarch in the Amanalla Elephant Camp, says Ramzan. Her life was

The KING and I

Waiting to see the tiger

saved only because the mahout had blunted the sharp end of his tusks, but the poor old cow was in great agony. I gaze uneasily at the massive beast, gently guided by the pressure of the mahout's toes positioned behind the animal's voluminous ears, and see no hint of his dark behavioural traits.

Indrajeet stops his descent into the *nullah*: he has reached his destination, and so have we. A little distance away is a family of five, one huge and four miniatures orange and black striped felines sprawled in a wedge between two rocks, shaded from the scorching sun. Three of the cubs are fast asleep — one with its paws up in the air — looking, deceptively, like innocent kittens taking a snooze. The mother appears to be unconcerned by the constant elephantine intrusions. One cub pushes himself forward, his little ears perked to attention, tiny tail stiff and alert. A low growl rumbles in his throat, he clearly dislikes our presence, and moves closer. In a flash, the mother snaps to attention, dismissing us with a chilling look before turning her attention back to the cub. She pins down her son, but once the 'Stay put' lesson is taught, she is all affection, her front paw draped across his shoulder, licking him constantly, a faint purr barely heard above the frenetic clicking of cameras.

Tigers, I know, make great mothers, protective, affectionate yet tough disciplinarians. Tiger moms are stay-at-home types, rarely straying away from the nursery, not venturing too far even to bring back dinner, which is why availability of prey base within the area is so important. Our little rebel has dozed off, snuggling against his mother's breast. My heart turns over, overwhelmed by the intense emotion I always feel when seeing the tiger.

'*Photo shooting finis?*' interrupts the mahout, directing his elephant to turn back. After all, for him it is all in a day's work, and he has other tourists to attend to. The pain of partition is almost physical as I tear myself away, but at the same time, I feel relieved. I had felt ashamed to drop in uninvited, intruding the cat family's peaceful slumber. It is a scene replayed everyday, hordes of holidaymakers parading incessantly, cameras trained on tigers — hunting, eating, crapping, mating; denying the animal even a vestige of privacy.

This is what wildlife tourism in India has become: tiger-centric. But nowhere else is it as maniacal as in Bandhavgarh. Touts guaranteed me a tiger when luring me to book a package, and the minute one arrives, the game starts. The waiter who woke me up, greeted me with, 'May you see tiger, Madam'. It has almost become a salutation, not unlike a 'good morning' greeting. That marked the beginning; each Gypsy we accosted had the same question, others had boastful answers, 'I saw one male, big, magnificent.'

I saw one too, female, beautiful, just the day before. But I wished I hadn't. She was a tiger walking on the road, padding serenely. In her stealth was grace and power, she glided along silently, like a golden phantom. There was no magic in this moment, for no sooner had we chanced upon her, another mad vehicle pounced in, chasing after the tigresses. She bounded off, melting into the undergrowth. I am not ashamed to say I lost my temper. This was the tiger's domain, we were mere guests. They had the right of way, not us. I reported the miscreants to the authorities, their entry was revoked, and the driver issued a stern warning.

But it is a lost battle. That same evening we go past the Amanalla camp, the sight of the morning tiger show. No tiger is within sight, just a convergence of vehicles, impatiently hoping for the animal to make an appearance. Our jeep pauses for a while, enough to make out that between morning and evening two cubs have crossed over to the other side. I can hear their plaintive meows, and the answering *auuuungh* of the mother. A cub cautiously steps on the road, then dashes back in, disconcerted by the avalanche that spreads before it. The tourist traffic has blocked the tiger corridor preventing the cubs from joining their mother.

I go away, most chose to wait the possible return of the cub. I am deeply distressed. I understand the importance of tourism as a source of revenue, for the park, the locals and the industry as a whole. Though locals do derive some benefit, tourism policy prevents revenue from ploughing back to the park. I appreciate that people must see tigers so that they are motivated to save them. It must be a rare person who is unmoved by a tiger in the wild.

But here I sensed no such awe in the company of the tiger, there was no drama, no uncertainty, just a badly mismanaged stage show, to ensure that merry-makers did not go back disappointed or feel cheated at not seeing the tiger. Rules, if not always rational, have been made to restrict pressure on the tiger, only to be broken. The tiger here appeared like a harassed Bollywood star, but unlike the latter the tiger did not hanker for such attention and publicity. He just wants his solitude, and peace.

How does this constant disturbance affect tigers? There are no studies, as far as I know, but I am convinced that the tiger cannot remain unaffected by this constant obsession. Gathering information from the beat guards over the next two days, I find that there is a general consensus that things have gone awry. An indicator I find most interesting is that tigers have apparently understood tourist timings. Forest guards on patrol say that the maximum sightings happen when the last jeep drives away. The King then takes over his jungle.

Bandhavgarh has a rich tiger history. It was in this park that Sita the tigress elevated the *Panthera tigris tigris* to its celebrity status. She was the star of many documentaries, and cover girl for National Geographic. Here she is worshipped like her Goddess namesake, wife of the Indian God, Ram. She is queen mother too, most of the striped felines we see in this park today are her progeny. The locals sing her paeans still, she was beautiful, graceful, the perfect

Left: Sita and her son (above)

mother, she was bold and apparently even her bone structure was flawless! She was a confiding soul, parading out at the sound of the vehicle; in those days tourism traffic had not reached this frenzied level. Sita was too beautiful, too trusting for her own good. She was killed. She is still beloved. Ten years after the incident, the guard who took me to the site where her leg had been trapped in a cruel steel jaw, burst into copious tears.

If Sita was loved for her beauty, then Charger was the legendary hero. Charger earned his name for his enthusiasm for dashing at practically every moving object. Tourist elephants were fair game, he attacked the rear end with seemingly deadly intention, traumatising those on board but giving them a great tiger tale to take back home. Charger never hurt anyone though, the mock charge appeared to be a game he hugely enjoyed. Visiting Charger Point, where the great cat lies buried, is almost a pilgrimage for each visitor, and even an annual Charger Cricket tournament has been institutionalised in his memory.

Given its past history, it is nothing short of a miracle that tigers still exist in this jungle. The tiger was the prized bag of sahibs and the Indian royalty, but the Maharajah of Rewa was particularly passionate about this bloodthirsty sport. As the story goes, a bag of 109 tigers was considered auspicious, and each successive king set out to achieve this number with diligence. Rajah Gulab Singh killed 144, of which 87 were shot in one calendar year.

The Rewa forests, of which Bandhavgarh is part, was also famous for its white tigers. It gave the world Mohan, the first known white tiger. A tigress was trapped in a beat along with her four nine-month-old cubs. All were shot, but the Maharajah of Rewa spared the white one owing to its ghostly pallor. That was Mohan, and he was used as a stud to breed white tigers. For this purpose, Mohan was housed in the summer palace of Govindgarh and yielded

Banka, Sita's son, licking his wounds

a succession of white tigers. Today, almost all the white tigers in the world, all in captivity, owe their genes to him. Contrary to popular belief, white tigers are not albinos but have retarded pigments and are what is called recessive mutants.

Among the present generation of tigers are B1, B2 and B3; one of whom was poached, another poisoned, a terrifying indicator that this tiger paradise has been tainted with blood. B3 is Charger's child, and has inherited his fathers' penchant for attacking vehicles. He is more fastidious; he only chases motorbikes, charging with ferocity and killer intent till the rider falls off his vehicle in terror. 'Once the man is down, waiting for Yamraj, the God of death, B3 walks away, without a backward glance, appearing as tame as a pussycat,' says a ranger, and a victim of this game.

As always, the tiger steals the show, as mega stars do. But the truth of the matter is, there is more to Bandhavgarh than the striped feline. Through the night, the Common Hawk Cuckoo or the aptly named Brainfever bird kept me

The *'Kurma'* or Tortoise *Avtar* of Vishnu

awake with her incessant call. Its song appealed to the Mughal emperors; Jehangir likened it to a 'soul-piercing lament', while the romantic Emperor Akbar wrote that the call 'makes love's unhealed wounds bleed anew'.

On the second night, I am interrupted by an urgent knock on the door. It's the *khansama* or the cook and he leads me to the edge of the garden where a barbed wire fences off the tiger reserve. It is pitch dark, though the moon and a thousand stars lit up the night. Beyond the borders, safe in its sanctuary, a plump sloth bear has seated itself next to huge termite mound. It is unaware of our presence, intent on gorging itself on ants, his favourite food. There is no accounting for tastes! I leave the bear to its feast, thrilled by my first sight of the bear in the wild. Till date, I had only seen them as dancing bears, bedraggled creatures, eyes glazed with pain, moving their bodies in a crazed frenzy, so removed from the free, wild species I saw today.

On my last day I walked up to the fort, set on an impressive plateau. Local lore has it that the plateau was flattened by Lord Ram's thumb, and the fort given as a gift to his brother, Lakshman. Hence the name Bandhavgarh, or brother's fort. It is said two architects from Hanuman's monkey army built the fort. The Baghel kings, the direct ancestors of the present Rewa royalty took possession of the fort in the twelfth century, and it remained their capital till 1617, after which it became their hunting preserve.

It is a beautiful walk, rich with historical and natural heritage. I pass ruins, which were once the boudoirs of queens, and stables that housed the King's horses and elephants. There's a rusted armoury, a decaying treasure house and a series of intricately carved temples. Most impressive, though, are the reservoirs of fresh water, thirteen of which dot the park. These

deep tanks remain full even during the driest summers. The top of the plateau is dotted with *Sinduri* trees, their bright red fruits a favourite of Malabar Pied Hornbills. I stationed myself next to the pond. Langurs dip their heads in the water; one bounds up and disturbs the peace of a dozen hornbills hidden amidst the green and red foliage. They explode into the air, their great yellow beaks seeming too heavy for them, their wings whooshing as they cut through the air. The hornbills disappear into the green of another tree. In the pond below, a freshwater turtle surfaces, raising its head cautiously before ducking back in. You could say it was just a turtle, or you may reverently

worship it as Kurma, the tortoise *avatar* of Lord Vishnu, a huge stone statue of which I just passed by. The fort also has statues of other incarnations of Vishnu – Varaha or boar, Matsya or fish and Narsingh or half-man, half-lion. God or animal? In India, both could be separate entities, or merge into one. Animals are worshipped as Gods: the elephant is Lord Ganesha, the monkey symbolises Hanuman, the boar is an incarnation of Lord Vishnu and the tiger worshipped as Baghdevta. I don't quite know how to explain this, but for one who has grown up in India, most animals wear a holy halo — from larger-than-life fauna like tigers and elephants, to the humble deer. The list of holy beasts even includes rats, snakes and our best friend, the dog. Here, the veneration is more intense, and may be attributed to the fusion of history, religion, mythology and nature, so perfectly merged in Bandhavgarh. In this land of God and nature, the peace is in stark contrast with the taxing tiger show of the previous day.

What, I wonder, is the truth of Bandhavgarh? Is the real jungle being obliterated by the ridiculous drama played out everyday? Yes, I accept the tiger as the protagonist must get its due, but there are other characters set in the wilds of Bandhavgarh. A bit of advice, even if unwanted. Avoid the theatre of the absurd, leave your feline sighting to chance and look beyond the tiger. Then, and only then, have you seen the real Bandhavgarh.

An Obituary

Once upon a time there lived a magnificent big cat. God was kind to this animal, He dressed it in ash-gold coat dappled with black spots. Awarded it good height, a tapering body and remarkable speed matched by no other. In His wisdom, God designed the cheetah in such a way that it would thrive with its tremendous burst of speed to down its meal. God, however, did not account for Man. That the very qualities the cheetah was endowed with for its own survival would also be its curse. That man would harness and use the speed for his own hunting games. That man would empty the wealth of the wild to fill his own coffers. Not satisfied with his employ, man made the cheetah the target of his gun as well. And so died the cheetah, fastest animal on earth, famous for its speed and agility, a product of millions of years of evolution. What follows is a short, if erratic, history of an extinct big cat.

The KING and I

I am particularly loath to write this belated obituary of a big cat, long departed, nearly forgotten. It's always a morbid task to chronicle the dead, but essential nonetheless as a grim reminder that extinction is not a prophecy of doomsday pundits, it occurs. It is forever. That while we pat ourselves on the back for conserving – but only just – the tigers and the leopards, the cheetah has crossed over to the netherworld. It was man who scripted the cheetah's obituary. We hunted it, destroyed its habitat and captured it for our macabre games, till no trace remained. The last record of the wild cheetah is in the same year we celebrated Independence and both were mired in the gory blood bath of the Partition in 1947. That, however, marks the end of the trail; our story starts at the beginning and carries through to its annihilation in an attempt to understand how planet earth's fastest animal lost its race to man.

I found my journey, this time restricted to yellowed tomes and research papers, archaic but fascinating. What triggered off my curiosity was an account I came across while preparing for a newspaper feature on the big cats of India. Jean de Thevenot, a French traveller records India in 1633, 'the great forests of Ahmedabad where they take panthers for hunting'. Till that day, more than a decade ago, I had little idea about the cheetah, except that no other animal could match its speed, and that it was gone. Dead. Extinct. The idea of a big cat both trained for hunting, and the target of a hunt intrigued me. But what amazed me was his description of Ahmedabad, the city where I grew up. Coursing with cheetahs in Ahmedabad? Could the ancient mariner be alluding to Ahmedabad, now a city well past its prime, its greens and grace choked and crippled with chaotic, effusive development? Alas, there are no great forests in the metropolis today, and it is impossible to imagine that there thrived enough game for the cheetah to hunt in my now concrete backyard.

As I read more I realised that, quite unwittingly, I had visited numerous places where the cheetah once lived and flourished. I lived in Baroda, now Vadodara, for years but was unaware that the city was an important centre of cheetah capture and coursing. In the early nineteenth century, the *Baroda Manual* laments that the 'population of cheetahs had diminished along with the diminished jungles'. Bhavnagar carried on the tradition of hunting with cheetahs well after independence, even if with imported stock from Africa. Dharamkumarsinhji, naturalist and scion of the princely state, wrote of 'one cheetah whose outstanding performance stands out above others. We have seen hunts by Hazur Prasad seldom failing'. I visited the palace but the memory of such a royal legacy was gathering dust under the staircase, a painting that showed a wild cheetah closing in on a blackbuck. Saranda and Palamau in Bihar were once the stronghold of the cheetah. Kutch, among my favourite destinations in Gujarat for its stark landscape, colourful people and intricate silver jewellery, is repeatedly noted in the history of cheetah hunts.

I went to the Melghat Tiger Reserve in Maharashtra once to follow a story of tiger poaching. Two tiger skins had been recovered, and stumbled on the fact that nearly one century before in 1890, three cheetah skins were seen in Melghat, according to one Mr. Burton. Another time, another species, same tragedy.

The cheetah, clearly, had a wide range across India. In appearance, the cheetah resembled a hound, so much so that for a long-time it was believed to be a dog-cat, a kind of cross between the two. There also existed the belief, no doubt owing to its swift stealth, that it was a bird of prey, soaring high to pounce on its prey. Scientifically, there is little doubt that *Acinonyx jubatus* is a cat, with numerous black spots, a black streak running down from the corner of each eye along the face; is taller than the leopard, has a remarkably small waist, legs slim and sinewy, claws semi-retractable: Perfectly designed to make it nature's most efficient sprinter.

God granted the cheetah prodigious speed to run down its prey. This specialised trait decreed that it lived in semi-desert areas, scrub jungles and grasslands of India where it could sprint with minimum obstruction. In 1867, T. C. Jerdon, surgeon in the Madras Army and author of *The Mammals of India*, traces its habitat throughout Central India, part of South India and through Sindh and Rajpootana to Punjab.

The cheetah's passage in India can be traced, though not with much accuracy to prehistoric rock paintings in the caves in Chambal Valley, Bhimbetka and Kahavai near Bhopal. There is some speculation of a Mohanjodaro seal depicting a cheetah-like animal.

The history of the cheetah is sketchy, and little has been recorded of its life in the wild. The animal was more celebrated by man as the Hunting Leopard. More pages have been devoted to the cheetah as a royal pet, employed for hunting.

The first definitive record of use of cheetahs for hunting appears in Sanskrit text, *Manasollasa*, which describes in flourishing detail the royal activity of *Vyaghraja*, where the deer is hunted with trained cheetahs. By the time *Manasollasa* was written in the twelfth century, coursing with cheetahs was an established tradition in court life, but it was in the

Previous page: Hunting with the Cheetah from *India and its Native Princes*; above: *The Hunting Cheetahs* by W. Daniells

period of the Mughal Empire that the cheetah came to occupy a prominent niche in imperial life. It also marked the beginning of its end. No other large cat had suffered such a fate: a systematic, continual removal from the wild to be designated as a hunter of antelope in the department of Imperial sports. This exercise lasted for many millennia and certainly diminished its stock in the wild.

Emperor Akbar was particularly passionate about the sport; he had during his reign about 9,000 cheetahs and at one point of time, his stables housed a thousand. Young Akbar was introduced to the cheetah for the first time in 1555 at the age of thirteen by the father of a courtier, 'a cita which had come into his hands from the Afghans and was called Fatehbaaz'. Akbar personally caught cheetahs; *Akbarnama* records the Emperor's sport near Gwalior in 1569 and 1571. His delight in the sport is extensively recorded. Akbar had his favourite cheetahs, who were accorded special honours. Samand Manik, for instance, was carried on a *chaudol* with much pomp. His servants ran on each side and a large drum beat in front. Citr Najan was another beloved cat.

Emperor Jehangir was equally fond of this sport and his memoirs, *Padshahnama* details many such hunts. Jehangir also gives us another insight to the animal. Cheetahs are believed to be prolific breeders in the wild, but in captivity cubs are rare. Akbar, apparently, tried hard to get his cheetahs to mate, even leaving them in pleasure gardens but to no avail. Eventually, of his menagerie of 9,000, writes Jehangir, a male slipped off his collar and went to pair with a female and three young ones were born!

The flamboyant hunting passion of the Mughals took its toll on the cheetahs but the hunt was not restricted to the Mughals alone. It continued with the Hindu princes; the Mewar school of painting depicts the Maharana of Udaipur coursing with the cheetah, as did Sawai Man Singh of Jaipur. Kolhapur was also famous for this sport, though by the time travel writer Sudyan Cutting witnessed the spectacle in 1948, the Maharajah had to import felid hunters from Kenya. By this time, the cheetah in India was almost extinct.

The prize trophy for the British was undoubtedly the tiger and the lion, the cheetah, too, was a marked cat. There are records of sahibs partaking in coursing with cheetahs. At the onset of the nineteenth century, it was clear that the sun had set on the cheetah. The *cheetahwalla pardhis* were giving up their traditional profession of trapping the big cat and taking to snaring birds and trapping deer. Dunbar Brander wrote that in the 1920s the number of cheetahs in the Central Province was negligible. R. I. Pocock recorded in 1939 that the cheetah was almost, if not quite, extinct in Hindustan.

The damning bullets were fired by Maharajah Ramanuj Pratap Singh Deo of the erstwhile state of Korea in Sarguja district in Madhya Pradesh in 1947. The ruler's private secretary writes in a note for the Bombay Natural History Society journal, 'All three cheetahs were shot by the Durbar in our state. He was driving at night and they were all sitting close to each other. They were all males, all in perfect condition. The first bullet killed one. The second bullet after having gone through one stuck the other and killed it also'. This was the last recorded occurrence of the cheetah in India. The cheetah had been wiped off. For ever.

The question of reintroducing the cheetah has been bandied about for years, since around the time we lost the cat. At the time, Iran had a healthy population of the Asiatic Cheetah: but latest reports indicate that just about twenty-five survive today and one might safely conclude that Iran is not going to be generous with them. Nor is reintroduction an easy task, and comes with its own share of problems. Also, is it prudent to reintroduce a species if the causes of extermination of a race persist? Cheetahs could obviously not be used to indulge in sport, but the grasslands they inhabited have been eroded by development. India's burgeoning population will not welcome a predator: its potential habitat has shrunk to negligible. As it is, the country is struggling to protect its other big cats from poachers, habitat destruction, human and livestock pressure.

The cheetah is now found in India only in the annals of history. I can only hope that a similar fate does not await our other big cats. That the children of tomorrow do not meet the tiger only in dusty libraries, rather than flourishing in the wilds…

African Cheetah

In the Footsteps of Carpet Sahib

Colonel Edward James Corbett earned fame as a hunter. He slayed troublesome tigers and leopards. The first was the Champawat man-eater, which killed 436 men. Corbett went on to bag many more, relieving the village folk of the terror that stalked their life. But Corbett maintained that the tiger was neither cruel nor bloodthirsty, just stressed by circumstances to adopt an alien diet. In the last twenty years of his life in India, he fought for the cause of wildlife.

He was a pioneer conservationist, rallying to save the tiger. 'A country's fauna is a sacred trust, and I appeal to all of you not to betray the sacred trust'. The Man-Eaters of Kumaon and his other books rich in jungle lore, are almost religious texts for me. Hence it was a given that I set out to explore Corbett country. As I followed his trail, I met a different Corbett, a sort of benevolent local rajah. People turned to Carpet saheb in times of trouble, he solved family disputes, calmed tensions between warring factions, provided good seeds and dispensed pills to the sick. Like the tigers he hunted, Corbett was a large hearted gentleman.

Jungle Story

'It was on a blistering hot day in May that I, my two servants, and the six Garhwalis alighted at Ramnagar and set off on our twenty-five-mile foot journey...'

Jim Corbett, *The Mohan Man-Eater*, 1944

It was a blistering hot day in May as well when I alighted at Ramnagar, albeit minus the aplomb. My modest entourage included just a photographer. The noble motive was also conspicuously missing; my mission lacked the hallowed purpose of rescuing a terrorised town from the wrath of a man-eater. My work was more like the hound in the hunt, nosing out and following the trail of the hunted: in this case Jim Corbett, the legendary hunter, a *pucca sahib* and pioneer conservationist.

I must confess that my trip had the trappings of civilisation. Not for me the twenty-five–mile foot walk; I whizzed past in a Gypsy, India's trademark jungle safari vehicle, to dump our luggage in the comfortable but rustic environs of Tiger Camp – our base for the Corbett trail – before making our way to Corbett Tiger Reserve, of which he was the true architect.

'If the Hailey Park is still there, I would like to go to Bijrani and take some photographs of tiger pugmarks'.

Jim Corbett, 1951, Kenya

The Hailey Park is still there, renamed Corbett as a memorial to the hunter and naturalist. Hunter he might have been, but Corbett was not reckless or extravagant with his shot. He used his gun to eliminate man-eaters and agitated about the declining wildlife of India, particularly tigers, 'When the tiger is exterminated as exterminated he will be unless public opinion rallies to his support...' It took a while in coming, but fortunately India, and the world, listened; shook off their apathy, abandoned the race to hunt trophies and devoted a conservation effort to pull back this endangered species. It survives, if only precariously.

Corbett's quarry escaped me here, but their presence was well advertised, tree trunks raked by claws and muddy paths imprinted with pugmarks. I noticed a clutch of white bones, all that remained of a cheetal, the tiger's dinner. The park is familiar territory to me, but this time I tried to look through Corbett's eyes. What would he have thought of the reserve? Would he have lauded the endeavour to conserve, or mourned the lackadaisical efforts to save wildlife? Our guide, Kunwar, gave us a point to ponder over: 'Times have changed since Carpet sahib,' he said 'no more man-eaters but tiger-eating men.' How true, tigers have preyed on man to assuage their hunger when hard pressed. Mankind is killing the beast now to sell and consume its bones. Pushing such macabre thoughts aside, I proceeded to the Garjia forest bungalow, where Corbett had once halted for a night. He lacked the necessary official permissions to avail its hospitality and was forced to sleep in the open. The resthouse is decaying and now serves as a liquor den for local louts. I fervently hoped this was not a sign of things to come.

Though rarely mentioned in his books, this is good elephant country. *Elephas maximus*, the world's largest land mammal, is yet another endangered species and my Corbett quest offered me a unique encounter with the elephant. I was at Dhikala, another forest resthouse built for weary British forest officials, and now a tourist hub. It overlooks the River Ramganga, and bears the notice: *Crocodiles in the river, survivors will be prosecuted*. I deliberated on this queer logic when an elephant ambled over to the dwindling river for a drink. She was a female, ardently pursued by a grand old tusker. It was evident that she was enjoying the attention, but didn't want to give in just yet. The courtship continued, trunks moved back and forth, touching, exploring. I absorbed the scene raptly, when a bellow filled the air. Another tusker, obviously also in the race for the lady's favours. He was young and brash and quickly made his move. What followed was a mammoth battle, the sound shook the earth, and the jungle trembled. It lasted only a few, eventful minutes, the older bull was emerging as a clear winner, and chastened, the contender backed out. The pair too moved away, fading into the sunset.

That night was devoted to elephantine encounters. A herd of pachyderms raided the camp at night, made straight for the canteen, thrashing and breaking all the barriers. Torches were lit, gunshots fired in the air to chase the elephants away. It wasn't a pretty sight, watching the majestic beasts shriek and run in terror. Ironic, I thought. Weren't we the intruders? Isn't it us humans who invade – unwanted and uninvited – their territory, their jungles, yet frighten them away when they come too close? Next morning, I headed for Mohan, my first station in Corbett's long list of slain man-eaters.

Corbett Country

'Was I a policeman? No. Was I a forest officer? No. Who was I? Just a man. Come to try and help the people of Mohan and Kartkanoula, by shooting the man-eater'

Jim Corbett, *The Mohan Man-Eater*, 1944

Mohan, once a hamlet in its infancy, has now grown to be a rather large village by the bed of the River Kosi. The Mohan man-eater had spread his terror wide, extending up to Katkinaav, more than 6,000 feet above. Corbett covered the twenty-mile range of the tiger on foot. It is said that he took only two days. From Mohan, Katkinaav is another 4,000 feet. It's picture-book pretty: a tiny collection of shops and houses all quite proud of their Corbett connection. The resthouse where the hunter stayed still exists, if in a run down manner and is perched on the ridge of a high hill. Our presence had attracted a motley crowd. Who was I? Why was I here? They didn't quite understand why I wanted to rake up dead tales, but, characteristically of all hill people, were generous with their time and information. And hospitable. Panna Devi offered me tea, while another robust young man persistently pushed for water. 'It is breast water, Madam,' he proclaimed. This was no sexual innuendo, I realised, it was rural India attempting Carpet Sahib's language. He meant 'best water'!

'*Bade shikari ka ghar hai, memsaab, kareeb 500 sher to maare honge,*' a local woman told me. It dawned on me that Corbett was a victim of his legacy, growing larger and more colourful with time. In the space of eight hours, the number of tigers' victim to Corbett's shot varied from 50 to 500. Corbett was no mere mortal. He had nerves of steel; he could

The KING and I

Ramganga River

shoot in the dark, halt a leopard mid-air, bagged tigers as big as elephants, and blindfolded at that. Leeladhar Bhatt, proprietor of a provision store in the Katkinaav market, appeared more pragmatic. He was a trifle disparaging about this Corbett affair but still found time from his brisk business to chat. He spoke of the man with studied dispassion, 'Mohan *sher* killed my *tai* (aunt). Then it ate two more women and Corbett was called.' Somewhere along the line, the romance of the tale took over. Corbett ensured an end to the terror. His estimation of Corbett's slain tigers was a neat hundred. Pratap, driver and Man Friday, is an old hand in these parts and advises us to take his words with a pinch of salt. 'Everyone here imagines a relationship to Corbett and his tigers,' he cautioned.

The 'Mohan Tiger' still roamed these parts. This one is a new-age tiger. He is not a man-eater. Quite the contrary, he's a gregarious guy with pious inclinations, he has been frequently sighted at a tiny temple a few miles beyond Mohan. How the times have changed!

'I offer it [Corbett's Kaladhunghi house] as a free gift to the Premier to be used as a panchayat house for Kaladhunghi'

Jim Corbett, 13 January 1952, Kenya

Corbett's home in Kaladhungi is – and God be thanked – not with the Panchayat, but an ode to the man. Letters, photographs and his personal effects are carefully preserved in the museum. His fishing rod and *sola* hat lay intact in a corner and faded photographs line the walls. No one can beat the government in making available inconsequential information. Inscribed under a photograph of Corbett standing over a dead tiger was the following caption: *Corbett used to go hunting in forest wearing an underwear, shorts and hat!*

Author at Katkinaav

There was also a picture of Robin: *Beloved dog and hunting companion.* The canine's grave had been given a makeover by the government. A monstrous steel structure had replaced the old gravestone. I love dogs, and found Corbett's writing on Robin particularly endearing, 'He was rising three months then and I bought him for 15 rupees. He is rising 13 years now, and all the gold in India would not buy him'. Devben Panwar, mentioned in

Corbett's home at Kaladunghi

The KING and I

Corbett's writings as Chota Panwa, had more to add on the sahib's indulgence for his dogs, 'He had three, and there was one man to feed them, another for bathing while a third would take them for walks'. More than anything else, it was the trees in the garden, which created the eerie Corbett-aura. These Litchi trees, gnarled with age were planted by Corbett and his sister, Maggie. They have lived and matured with the family and one wonders what they would say if they could speak.

'Give to Bahadur and my other friends in Kaladhunghi my best salaams. I am still with them, and that they must not be anxious about anything. When we are quite well we will go back to Kaladhunghi.'

Jim Corbett, 24 March 1948, Kenya

In a way, Chota Haldwani, a tiny village in Kaladhunghi's backyard, still awaited Carpet Sahib's return. The Corbetts owned this tiny village when they left India and gifted it to their tenants. Here we met a different Corbett. Not just the fearless hunter, but also a sort of local Raja, benevolent and generous.

For Corbett enthusiasts, the village is a gold mine; the land is his, and so are the people. There was Chota Panwa, who delivered milk and curd to Carpet Sahib's house every Sunday, and always got something in return. A *paisa* or two, or unfamiliar delights like cakes and

Corbett with a slain man-eater

patties from the kitchen. 'No one ever went back empty-handed from Sahib's house. Maggie memsahib saw to that,' he reminisced. His father, Bada Panwa, knew the sahib well, counseled him on property matters and in typical native fashion worried about Carpet Sahib's bachelor status. 'He was also very concerned about Maggie memsahib. She also bachelor, not good for woman,' he advised.

Further inside the village lived Khimori Devi, bent with age, and the burden of living. 'I am waiting,' she said, 'for God to take me. So I can be at peace.' Her empty eyes lit up at the mere mention of Corbett. His mention infused her with life. She hobbled inside and returned with a single barreled muzzle-loader gun. Khimori Devi was the proud owner of the hunter's legacy; Corbett gave one of his rifles to her husband, the late Sher Singh. Tears flowed freely as she remembered the sahib, her frail arms hugging the gun, and all that it symbolised. *Carpet sahib ki sarkar achchi thi, ab hum anath hai,*' she mourned. 'When he was here, we had no worries. The moment he realised any of us had a problem he took

Robin

The KING and I

care of it, whether it was an illness or a leopard who ate our goats. Sahib was very fond of Trilok *ke* papa (my husband). If he were ill, saheb would bring medicines and send fruits and meat. In good times, he was one of us, dancing in Baisakh (harvest festival) and weddings. He loved to fish and he always kept a share of the catch for us.'

'*Bada khana bhi hota tha.* [Christmas]. We all used to go to his house for a feast. We never paid taxes even after he gave us the land and left India, the money order used to come from Kenya. He said he will come back.' Her voice trailed off, and when we got up to leave, she grabbed my hand to point to the wall encircling the village. It was built by Corbett to protect the fields from straying, marauding animals. I left her, huddled in a corner, clinging on to a legacy worn thin by time. Carpet sahib will never die here, he is immortal...

St John's Church

'*Pick up the map of India, run your eye straight up into the foothills of the Himalayas in the north of the United Provinces. There you will find Naini Tal, the summer seat of the Government of United Provinces, packed from April to November with Europeans and wealthy Indians seeking escape from*

Corbett's mother's grave

Jim Corbett

the heat of the plains, and occupied during the winter only by a few permanent residents, of whom most of my life I was one… '

Jim Corbett, *My India*, 1952

Nainital, Corbett's summer abode, was the thorn in the trail. Corbett's association with Nainital runs deep; he spent his school days here and served on the Municipal Board. But as we ascended to the hill station, I wondered whether Corbett would still want Nainital as his summer home? No, I was convinced, as I looked at the hideous holiday retreats that defaced the slopes. Game seen around the town as mentioned in his books, has now vanished. *Man-Eaters of Kumaon* and other books authored by him are best sellers in the Mall, but when we asked our way to his home, Gurney House, I drew a blank. Nainital, it seems, had wiped Corbett from its memory.

Gurney house was a beautiful old bungalow and well-preserved. It's still in the possession of the Verma family, who bought it when Corbett left for Kenya for Rs 50,000, well below the market price. I peered through the dusty glass pane and made out a grand old piano (Maggie used to play, if I remembered correctly). I could see deer trophies as well, had they been killed by Corbett? Here, too, Corbett's heritage was endangered. Gurney House was up for sale, it had been awaiting a buyer for the last two years. I imagined it falling prey to a greedy builder, who would reduce history to shambles and resurrect a fancy resort on its ashes. I shuddered. An old man walking down the road shared my grief. He is part of that history, he remembered Corbett as the sahib who always had coins and sweets for the children on the street, of whom he was one.

Sacred to the memory of Mary Jane Corbett. Born 12th March 1837. Died 16th May 1924. Until the day break and shadow fall away…

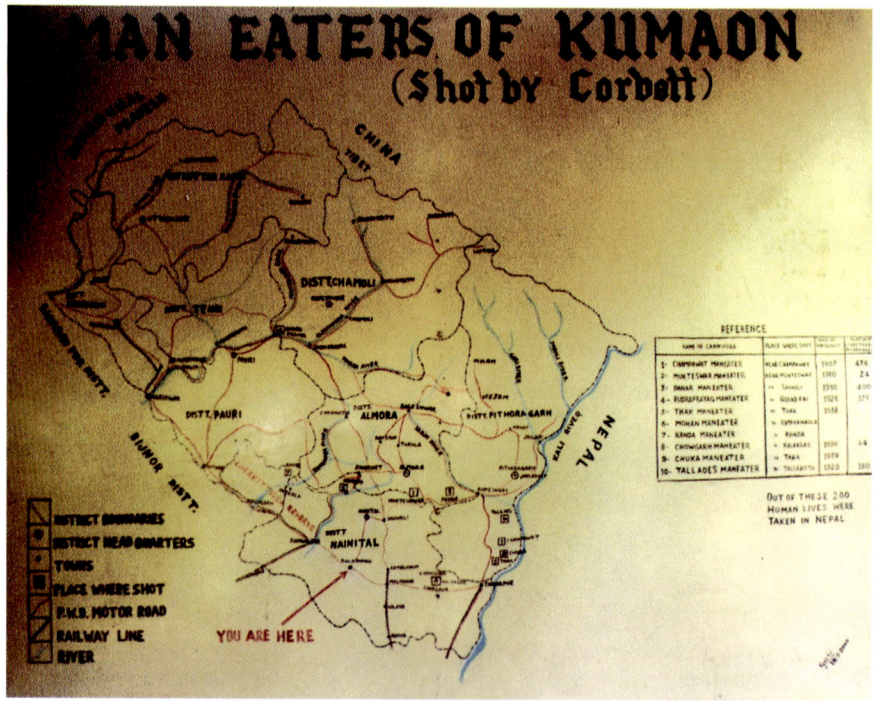

It was the decayed graveyard at St John's Church that made Nainital worthwhile. Here, among the hundreds of graves, lost beneath dirt and filth lay the mortal remains of Corbett's mother. Ruffians had made the yard their home, and looking at the filth, the debris, and gamblers, I almost gave up before I started. I sifted through years of grime and dust and pushed aside stinking unmentionables in an attempt to discover the grave of Corbett's mother (take heart, dear traveller; this need not be part of your itinerary). Fortune favours the brave, for a dusty three hours later I found her grave. Mary Jane Corbett, mother of Jim Corbett. My elation would not have been greater had I unveiled a pot of gold.

'People who lived at Mukteswar claim that it is the most beautiful spot in Kumaon, and that its climate has no equal. A tigress that thought as highly of the amenities of Mukteswar took up her residence in the extensive forests adjoining the small settlement...'

Jim Corbett, *The Mukteswar Man-Eater*, 1954

The tiger had it right, this tiny hill station three hours from Nainital is unbeatable in its beauty and climate but no tiger in its right mind would venture near Mukteshwar now. The jungles have thinned and the King still fears the gun. We reached at dusk and made a ritualistic visit to Badri Lal's orchard, where Corbett killed the Mukteshwar man-eating tiger.

Badri Lal has since died and his assorted heirs have migrated to more lucrative environs, there was little that remained of the past.

We headed back to camp. It was cold, and we huddled around the campfire. Locals dropped by with their tales of shikar. Spiced up jungle encounters grew bigger and more unbelievable with each sip of beer. Did I know of the tiger, which fell from a tree onto the shikari? Or of the man who is supposed to have killed no less than a 1,000 big cats? Of course, the tales were too fantastic to be true, but hunting, I thought with sorrow, was still considered a macho game. It was still a way of life here and the law had little meaning. In this part of the country, everyone fancied himself to be a Jim Corbett, if not one step ahead. They had it wrong; Corbett was never a willful hunter, he picked up his gun only to wipe out troublesome tigers. 'A man-eater is a tiger that has been compelled by circumstances to adopt an alien diet. Stress, in nine cases out of ten wounds, and in the tenth, old age'. His joy at easing the terror of an afflicted region was accompanied, in no less measure, by sorrow at bringing to end a magnificent beast. He worried that the instances of man-eating and cattle lifting were increasing due to the unrestricted slaughter of game, that had disturbed the balance of nature. In his later years, he shot with the camera, not the gun. For Corbett, like the tigers he so loved, was a large-hearted gentleman.

And then there were none...

Sariska is not a traveller's tale in the strict sense of a weekend escape from Delhi. For many years, it held pride of place as the closest forest to the Indian capital where the tiger roamed. I have often used this park as a convenient, relaxing getaway and it had always complied, but was my last visit a journey into the 'Valley of Death', a sojourn to a tiger reserve without tigers? The following chapter is an account of my search for the tiger in Sariska in early 2005, as part of the official team that went over the reserve with a toothcomb, post reports that Sariska had no tigers. Need I add that it was a futile, heartbreaking task?

Once upon a time, there was a rich and fecund forest, nestled beneath the bosom of the scenic Aravalli range. The King, Sher Khan, the Royal Bengal Tiger then ruled Sariska. He was its undisputed monarch; his roar or a hint of his presence sent his subjects—the leopard, deer, monkeys and peacocks scurrying for cover. But even in their primal fear they knew that the tiger's occurrence in the jungle was vital. Indeed crucial for he controlled the population of the herbivores, ensuring that they did not eat themselves out of their home.

Then one day, the jungle ceased to vibrate with his roar and silence reigned supreme. There were no furtive games of life and death between the hunter and the hunted. The King had died but his prey did not rejoice, for they realised that the jungle would follow thereafter.

In the May of 2004, the forest department decreed that sixteen to eighteen tigers roamed the forests of the Sariska Tiger Reserve. There was no reason to disbelieve them; a friend had recently witnessed a tiger treeing a leopard, while another came back thrilled that a tiger, offended at his peace being disturbed, had chased his jeep. I have never seen the big cat in Sariska, but my experience here was particularly reassuring. Once, while on my way out of the park, the jeep was halted by a frantic rustle in the bushes, accompanied by the terrifying bellow of two tigers. The roar filled the air, split the sky. The earth trembled. The jungle was vacant as far as the eye could see, for the other forest denizens had melted away in awe and fear. The tigers were mating, perpetuating their kind. I left them to their job, happy to know that the forest was to witness a new generation of tigers. Little did I know, then, that the cubs would be stilled even before they left their mother's womb.

The KING and I

The coupling of tigers is an interesting affair. I remember reading that the actual act lasts no more than twenty seconds, though they may repeat it every fifteen minutes. The tigress is quite demanding and her male may be expected to copulate fifty times over a couple of days. The impotent human male, foolishly believing that he can acquire similar prowess, seeks his cure in the penis of the tiger. The tiger penis soup is easily, if illegally, available in the streets of Far Eastern markets. Searching for the tiger in Sariska some five years later, I wondered sadly if this lust for tiger penis and other body parts that had made the big cat extinct here. Had the tigers I encountered been butchered, boiled down to soup and consumed in some corner café on an unknown street of an unidentified country?

As the new year dawned in 2005, alarm bells started ringing in Sariska. The tigers had gone missing and none had been sighted since July 2004. In less than a year all sixteen tigers had been wiped off these forests, marked for their protection. The administration, from Project Tiger Directorate downward, was in a panic. Letters and faxes dashed back and forth between Delhi, Jaipur and Sariska and urgent meetings were convened. A plan to search for the missing tigers of the beleaguered reserve was hastily drawn up and 280 forest guards and trackers went on a live tiger hunt, combing the forest for any signs of the cats. The officials put on a brave front while they tried to keep the tiger alive on paper, citing vague reports of a sighting, of fresh scat being found. But in their eyes and in the barren forest I read the truth — the king was dead.

Maharaja Jai Singh

Sariska was done with its days of glory. Once, this tiger-rich forest was the favourite haunt of hunting royalty. Way back in 1876, the French traveller, Louis Rousselet wrote of bagging 'a very fine tiger' in the gorges of the Aravallis, in a hunting excursion with the 'Ulwar' king, Maharao Rajah Sheodan Singh. In the early nineteenth century the hunting stories took a more colourful and gory shade.

My base for the tiger pursuit (fruitless) was the Sariska Palace, a hotel remodeled from the old hunting palace built by Maharajah Jai Singh in 1938. The Maharajah's hunts were stuff legends are made of. They were perhaps the most elaborate in India; he turned the shikar into a military exercise using whole battalions and the entire cavalry to drive tigers and other game towards the waiting guns. At other times, he lured the prey to his home. Goats were tied atop a table in the centre of a walled garden and leopards and the occasional tiger would saunter in for an easy meal, only to fall to a hail of bullets. If Jai Singh was so inclined, he would use elderly widows and small children as baits for the tiger. His rationale, when remonstrated by the British Resident, was 'I never miss!'

There was neither time nor the inclination to dwell on such bloodthirsty stories, enriched by time and re-telling. Sariska was in the grip of a tiger calamity, though first impressions suggested otherwise.

The forest is rich with tiger prey. Cheetal daintily mince through the grass. Ungainly *nilgai*, with ludicrous goatees, are conspicuous by their presence. A magnificent male

A royal shoot

The KING and I

sambhar lowers his impressive crown of antlers and sprays himself thoroughly with urine, an exercise that inexplicably makes him irresistible to the doe. I spot peafowl waddling towards a waterhole. While the hens drink and incessantly pick worms off the ground, the lone male follows, executing his elaborate courtship dance, spreading his vibrant fan wide. He struts and he sways but while the spectacle leaves me thoroughly enamoured, it fails to impress the hens for whom it is intended. The scene is peaceful, almost too peaceful, I fancy. I imagine serenity in the eye of the deer, the prey freed of the terror of the predator.

I surveyed all the tourist routes; to the Pandu Pol temple, ranked high in the pilgrim calendar owing to the legend that the Pandavas (protagonists of the *Mahabharata*) played their game of dice here that lead to their exile. Another story claims that the monkey God Hanuman punched his way through the mountain leaving a gaping hole, much revered today by the devoted.

Religion did not occupy my mind for the moment, my interest lay solely in the Late Pandu Pol tiger, one of the most frequently sighted cats in recent years. He stalked a vast territory, roaming over much of the reserve and the guards took to calling him Field Director sahib. "He did the job of the Field Director, patrolling the park," extolled Udai Ram, the ranger. Expectedly, his forays led the 'FD' into many a battle, he strayed into the territory of other tigers, dallied with their women and got into fights with other males who defended their land and mates. He carried the scars of many a combat and lost an eye. He earned himself a new sobriquet, Rana Sanga, the one-eyed battle weary Rajput royal. Not only was it more appropriate, the guards probably did not want to risk equating an injured warrior with

Waterhole

their boss! Rana Sanga has disappeared off the face of Sariska since the past year. As has Boxer, the young male of Kalighati. Boxer was an aggressive tiger prone to brawl with his kind. He did not like humans either and stories abound of his mock-charging straying jeeps. The game is over, Boxer has lost his fight with man; he is now just another statistic on the missing list of tigers. Through the day, I hear of other tigers and their tales, all with the same postscript: it has gone, madam, the tiger is no more. Tragically, all tiger stories in Sariska are authored in the past.

Next day, on February 4, 2005, I join the search party. Hard facts are discouraging; the animal has not been sighted for over six months. For four days, beginning February 1, about 300 people have been

Top: Looking in vain for pugmarks and tiger pugmark cast (above)

searching for a trace of the tiger in one of the smallest of India's tiger reserves. Each day they come back, despair and hopelessness writ large on their faces. The tiger, by all accounts, has vanished without a trace.

I am joined in the tiger quest, or rather I am tagging along with a senior park official, whose name I must not take since I am there unofficially. For the purpose of convenience he is CF, Conservator of Forests. Also with us is Ram Karan, an expert tiger tracker who has been on the job for the past nine years. Hope, they say lies eternal and it flutters faintly in my breast. I begin with a prayer on my lips. Each visit to tiger country is accompanied by a fervent wish to see the tiger. This time, there is desperation in my plea. Any sign, a pugmark, scratch, kill or scat would be a blessed event for it would make the difference between life and death for the tiger in Sariska.

Our tracking begins at Ghan ka tiraha, where the CF notices the smelly entails of a recent kill complete with drag marks. A carnivore has been at work, but not *the* carnivore. Evidence shows that it was a hyena. We move on, hope lends a spring to our steps and the forest made our march easy. Sariska has a raw beauty, it is a scrub forest with thick undergrowth that make it perfect habitat for the peafowl and is drably decorated with dry leaves of the *dhok* tree, interrupted by sudden bursts of green indicative of a pool closely. The waterbody is called Chhanpipda, where a tigress gave birth and brought up her cubs four years ago. Another of Sariska's missing tigers, not seen since 2002.

It's a steep hike, we have to climb 1,500 feet to reach our destination, the Gham Plateau. Our progress becomes slow, not only because of my inexperience in such uneven terrain but also because we keep a careful eye on any possible sign of the tiger. Deep incisions in the ground seem cat-like but they are caused by the sambhar. A tuft of hair, orange highlighted by black and roots of white has me in feverish excitement but to no avail. Cheetal, concludes Ram Karan. I gather that anxiety makes our imagination work overtime. By now we have reached the plateau.

One possible explanation offered for the tiger's absence is that it may still be residing in the higher reaches. In Sariska, during monsoons when water is plenty, the big cats prefer to live in the hills where disturbance from tourists and pilgrims is minimal. As the winter sets in and water dries up, they move to the valleys below and are easily sighted. This theory falls flat. The waterholes are bone dry and prey base almost negligible, aside from a herd of sambhar who panic at our arrival. Why would any tiger choose to stay here when a virtual feast awaits him in the gorges below? We have walked for five hours, covering the core area of the park and not come across the faintest trace.

Instead, what are visible are the confident pugmarks of a pair of leopards. A close investigation shows that it is a couple, Mr and Mrs Leopard out for a stroll. I can almost hear our hearts sink, collectively. Not that, I hasten to add, I have anything against the leopard, quite the contrary. But this, if nothing else, is the surest, almost definitive signal that there

The Leopard has taken over...

Sariska Hunting Lodge

isn't any tiger in these parts. Tigers can easily make mincemeat of their smaller cousin and may do so given an opportunity, for it considers the leopard a risk to its cubs and competition for its food. No leopard would dare tread without fear in the tiger's domain, like our friends seem to have done. A little ahead are the pugmarks of yet another leopard and I am informed that sightings of *Panthera pardus* are on the increase.

By now the awful truth has begun to sink in, there are no tigers in Sariska. You could contradict the statement, for I devoted only a morning to the exercise and covered only a part of the park. But the hopeless news brought in by trackers, coupled with my barren trail, convinced me that the King of beasts had ceased to be. There was no joy in our descent back to the valley; anguish had engulfed anticipation.

Inane thoughts crept into my mind — the official jeep we had come in was referred to as Tiger II, will it now be renamed? A guidebook I had referred to in my previous visit informed that 'Sariska was one of the best places to view the tiger and daytime sightings were on the increase'. Will those lines be now rewritten? Ram Karan, who was brought up in the adjoining village of Amra ka Vas, told me that they loved to sneak into the jungle when they were young to eat *ber* (jujube) that grew abundantly here. But they were scolded by the elders, "*Jungle mein nahar hai, bach ke rehana*" Beware, there are tigers in the forest. Would Ram Karan warn his kids anymore, when there are no tigers to dread? Ironically his work entailed protecting the tiger. Soon he could be out of a job; there were no tigers to save.

I dare not think of the ecological repercussions, of the health of a forest denied its top predator: It was the beginning of the end for the reserve. I dare not mourn our utter failure to protect our national animal. I dare not think of the end they might have met, in a poacher's death trap or shot through the heart by a gun.

I could only grieve for the tiger, now extinct from Sariska.

The official verdict came later, much after my visit, and following a series of inquiries. So shaken was the country by the plight of the tiger that the Prime Minister stepped in, ordering a CBI (Central Bureau of Investigation) inquiry. The report confirmed that there were no tigers in Sariska, all that remained had been poached, while the department slept on, unaware, unmindful of the carnage in their backyard. Local poachers had killed the tigers, mostly by iron and steel jaw traps that clamped on the tiger's paw. The animal was put out of its agony by either a bullet or a spear thrust into its mouth, to avoid blemishing its coat. The tigers of Sariska had all been sold to Sansar Chand, the most dreaded and notorious name in wildlife trade.

Sansar Chand

Will Sariska teach us a lesson? Somehow, I think not. My exit from the reserve is marked by the news of big wildlife product seizure in Delhi, including tiger and leopard skins and body parts. I do not think I will go to Sariska again. The shame and guilt of being a human, part of a race that saw the gory end of another is a burden too hard to bear. Adieu, *Panthera tigris tigris*, I hope your time in the nether world is gentler than the home that was your fate on earth.

Quo Vadis Panthera tigris tigris?

In the twenty-five years that preceded and followed the nineteenth century, more than 80,000 tigers were slaughtered in India. Laudatory, was the general presumption. Tiger was vermin, best exterminated. One dead animal could fetch Rs 5 to Rs 25. Tiger was good trophy too, hunted by royals and sahibs. Post Independence, the carnage continued. Amidst this senseless butchery, alarm set in the 1960s. The tiger was vanishing. Thus began a crusade to protect the tiger, which took on the official form of Project Tiger, the world's biggest conservation initiative, launched in Corbett National Park in April 11, 1973. Will Project Tiger succeed, mused naturalist M. Krishnan at the birth of the initiative. Three decades of Project Tiger, and we are nowhere close to an answer. The tiger still lives, but the tiger is dying as well, shamefully slayed for commerce. Its continued slaughter has put a question on its future. This chapter follows the tiger's chequered history, provides an insight into the current tiger crisis, questions the success or failure of the efforts to save the tiger and ponders over its fate.

Unreal as it seems now, there was a time when it was a toss up between humans and tigers. Referring to the early part of the eighteenth century, naturalist Dunbar Brander pondered: 'At one time in parts of India, tigers were so numerous it seemed to be a question as to whether man or tiger would survive,' 150 years later it is clear that *Panthera tigris tigris* is losing the battle. The 40,000-odd tigers at the turn of the nineteenth century had plummeted to a mere 1,800 by 1969. There are many reasons for this. For one, its jungles were dismembered. Another was 'sport.' Pre-independence, the tiger was the prized trophy for the Indian royalty. Shooting a tiger announced the coming of age for young princes, as did a sexual dalliance with a courtesan. Bagging a tiger and a woman made a boy a man. A true rite of passage!

The KING and I

Trophies on display

The Maharajah of Sarguja was the record holder, with over 1,100 heads under his belt, while the Rewa kings considered it auspicious to kill 109 tigers once anointed on the throne. Paradoxically, the tiger was 'protected', reserved only for the royal gun. If the common man poached in the royal preserves or even stole a blade in the tiger's jungle, he could be condemned to death. Then the sahibs came, and, along with the rest of India, they conquered its tigers. It was the ultimate trophy.

Arranging a tiger shoot was one of the finest ways to win friends and influence people in high places and royalty curried favour from the British by arranging elaborate hunts. The Raj also adopted another destructive step – the systematic annihilation of tigers as pests with a bounty in most of its range, for instance, in Mysore, the hunter was awarded Rs 25 for a dead tiger. Leopard and wild dog were also treated as vermin.

In a free India, the prerogative of the royalty and the sahibs turned into a happy hunting ground for anyone who owned a gun – from the dollar tourists to the local hero with a *desi katta*. Nets were laid, traps set, shots fired, trees chopped, forests burnt. Even the successful induction of forest officers was marked by a tiger hunt. Another deathblow was the skin trade; the tiger skin coat was the ultimate luxury fashion statement in the western world and it made a fancy rug. The scale was enormous, in a survey by the first Project Tiger director, Kailash Sankhala saw hundreds of tiger skins and rugs for sale, and export, in the markets of Delhi. The tiger was doomed.

A Status Report

Then the endangered big cat found a powerful saviour in the late Prime Minister, Indira Gandhi. When advised of the precarious position of the tiger, she took up the cause with a personal zeal, silencing the demands of a dollar-hungry shikar lobby, 'We need foreign exchange, but not at the cost of the life and the liberty of some of the most beautiful inhabitants of this continent.' She enforced a ban on tiger shooting and commercial sale of tiger derivatives, piloted the Wildlife Protection Act (1972) and the Forest Conservation Act (1990) and spearheaded the birth of Project Tiger in 1973. Nine tiger reserves were declared to protect 16,399 sq kms of feline habitat. The reserves were sacrosanct. Worldwide support poured in and the cause was taken up by devoted officers. The tiger made a comeback. Their numbers doubled to 4,000 in the next 15 years.

One morning the euphoria died. The celebrations of two decades of Project Tiger in 1993 were marked with despair. Wild tigers were being massacred to feed the demand for skins and bones. Eight tiger skins and 400 kg of bones were seized in August that year. Just one brewery in Taiwan was illegally importing 2,000 kgs of tiger bone and the source for raw material was India. The impact of this macabre trade was felt in Ranthambhore in Rajasthan, where numbers crashed from a healthy forty-five to less than twenty. It was not just Ranthambhore; tigers had gone missing in Sariska, Dudhwa and other reserves.

Circa 2004. Sinister, the way the tragedy is being replayed. The tiger is extinct in Sariska. A CBI inquiry into the tragedy confirmed that local poachers had killed the tigers of Sariska

and sold them. Skins, bones, whiskers, blood – nothing had been wasted. Now, they couldn't find any more tigers to harvest.

Bandhavgarh has lost many tigers, Panna is facing a tiger drought as well, though officials are still in denial mode. There are other stories, equally tragic. Dampha is beyond redemption, as is Buxa. Not a pugmark seen, not a single cattle kill — indicators of a dwindling tiger population. Sightings in Dudhwa, with over hundred 'official tigers' in Uttar Pradesh, are low. I went there last year, and an intensive three-day tour in the park did not yield any clue to the big cats' presence. Palamau suffers from a severe Naxalite problem, officials work there at constant risk to their life. A forester, attempting to protect the park and its tigers, had his head chopped off. He is just one among many such victims. Indravati in Chhatisgarh is a similar story, as is Nagarjunasagar in Andhra Pradesh. Hunting is a time-honoured tradition in Namdapha Tiger Reserve in Arunachal Pradesh, and again, the number of these big cats present there is anybody's guess.

Though the catastrophe appears sudden, it is not so. It is doubtful that the reserves had the stated numbers in the first place. Tigers existed, but only in the imagination, and files, of park officials. I am not even questioning the pugmark census method, though it has many detractors. The undisputed fact is that most park directors conjure up imaginary tigers to show a higher population; it avoids unpleasantness, inquiries, keeps their job safe and creates a feeling of false security. Except for the species concerned. In Ranthambhore, the 2004 census showed a healthy forty-seven, by next year the numbers were a mere twenty six. Some had died naturally. Others met a gory, untimely death. Some never existed at all. Last year's census in Sariska professed sixteen to eighteen tigers. The CBI report on Sariska stated that census numbers were grossly inflated. Whatever the numbers might have been, now there are none…

The most obvious culprit in this horrifying decline is poaching. The year 2004 saw the biggest seizure of the last decade in Tibet of 39 tiger and 579 leopard skins, all sourced from India. There has been a spate of seizures thereafter, including one in January 2005 in Delhi, where two tiger skins, sixty kilos of tiger bones, leopard paws and fourteen tiger canines were found. At least sixty tigers have been killed, post Sariska. The knowledge that our national animal is being decimated appears to have made little impact besides the usual perfunctory noises. The hunt is still on, the western world covets striped skins for coats and rugs, while the Far East brews bones to cure an ailing ulcer or a sagging libido. Wildlife crime is an organised, lucrative business, second only to drugs in terms of value. Intelligence information reveals that this bloody trade finances terrorism worldwide.

The other insidious threat to the tiger is the extirpation of its habitats. India has lost over fifty per cent of potential tiger habitat since she gained independence. Land is premium and the only land in India which has not been used, or abused, is forestland. Everyone covets it – builders, miners, industrialists, politicians, farmers – and will bend every law in the book to claim it.

Reserves have also lost their holy status and have been invaded by destructive development projects. Sariska has been ravaged by soapstone and marble mining; three nuclear reactors are planned near the Sunderbans, Nagarjunasagar and Kanha respectively, while Sunderbans and Corbett have been earmarked for a grandiose, ecologically suicidal tourism project. Part of Melghat was de-notified to make way for a power project, a tiny part of Periyar must give way to a temple and a battle to plough a road through Corbett rages on.

Even as there is a hue and cry about the tiger crisis, the ground reality remains unchanged. If anything, the pressures and threats worsen, everyday. Most tiger reserves are understaffed by thirty per cent, and due to freeze in recruitment, most of the existing staff are too old and unfit to handle the physical demands of the job. Plus, they are poorly equipped with defunct weapons and suffer from a total lack of basic infrastructure, like paucity of funds for diesel to fill patrolling jeeps. Conviction rate of wildlife crime is lower than one per cent.

The bigger tragedy is that the government and Project Tiger barely recognise the current crisis even in the face of overwhelming evidence. Hiding behind bureaucratic talk and diplomatic answers does not help matters. But one would stop short of laying the blame solely on the door of Project Tiger. With all its faults, and there are plenty, the biggest success

The KING and I

of Project Tiger has been that it has saved, against all odds, a species condemned to extinction by the end of the century. It has resurrected doomed forests and by protecting the tiger's habitat the project has served as an umbrella under which numerous other species survive. Like the Swamp Deer, whose extinction was imminent when the protection accorded to Kanha and Dudhwa saved it.

The problem is that Project Tiger itself is like a tiger sans teeth. It funds reserves across the country, but has little authority over them. The directors are appointed at the discretion of the state government, and rarely do the funds released by the authorities reach the reserves. The money is routed through the state exchequer, and in most cases that's where it stays. For example, Manas in Assam was sanctioned Rs 1.79 crores in 2003-2004 but the park received only 39 lakhs, that too only by the end of the year. One fallout was that daily wage labourers could not be paid. And this, in one of the parks besieged by militants and poachers. Rhinos have been wiped out, tuskers are very rare and tigers have been reduced to unknown numbers. The poachers didn't spare the foresters, either. In the past six years, poachers have killed eleven guards in Manas. Can one expect forest guards to protect the tiger when they are uncertain about their next meal and their future? Is it even morally correct to pat ourselves on the back about the 'great tiger success story' and discuss concerns in hi-flying international conferences when the ground reality is so abysmal? Manas is not the only park denied funds sanctioned to it; even high profile ones like Corbett are not spared. In states like Bihar, Assam, Rajasthan, Tamil Nadu and Arunachal Pradesh funds are not released or are delayed for months.

A Status Report

The fate of the tiger lies in the hands of a battery of disjointed, disinterested state governments, who place the national animal at the bottom of their priority list, if at all. The system rots. Good officers rarely last and are hastily transferred by politicians interested in getting those ready to fill their coffers and bend to their will.

One of the most serious concerns is that the tiger, or indeed the forests and wildlife, have no political support at all. In a press conference, the current Minister of Environment and Forests, Thiru A. Raja waxed eloquent about putting in place a speedy system for giving clearances to mining, industrial and other developmental projects in sanctuaries and forest areas. His knowledge on issues concerning wildlife bordered on the ridiculous. He, and an equally ignorant journalist, discussed at length the issue of reopening of trade in *shahtoosh* as proposed by the Jammu and Kashmir government, which were the 'feathers of an endangered bird, the chiru'. Mr Minister, here's news for you. The 'chiru' is endangered all right, but it is a mammal, not a bird and there is an ongoing international campaign to stop the illegal slaughter of about 10,000 animals each year.

In the war against wild India, state governments are campaigning hard with Maharashtra and Madhya Pradesh leading the battle to dilute the Forest Protection Act, 1980, which essentially prohibits use of forestland for commercial purposes and is widely accepted as the one law that has proved to be a saviour of our forests. The honourable Prime Minister may have ordered a CBI inquiry into the Sariska crisis, made a token visit to Ranthambhore and set up a Tiger Task Force (TTF) to look into the crisis, but how sincere and effective are such moves? What use are high-powered committees when his government is busy playing vote bank politics, which will ensure the death of wilderness in India? The government has drafted a bill entitled 'The Schedule Tribes and Forest Dwellers (Recognition of Forest Rights) Act, 2005', which if it comes through will ensure the end of every bit of wilderness in India. Effectively, the law will redistribute

The KING and I

forestland to tribals, and India will lose over sixty per cent forest cover. Once forestland comes under private ownership as the Bill proposes, the land mafia will move in. It's a moot point whether tribals will benefit. The spread of civilisation into wilderness has shown that the symbiotic relationship between forests and tribals is a myth. The day of the hunter-gatherer tribal is over, tribal societies have been exposed to consumerism, though they lack purchasing power.

Opening up of the forest, land, trees, timber, forest produce, with no law enforcement in place will simply lead to exploitation, and ultimate death of the forest. There is simply too much money in exploiting forests and killing tigers to do away with the law governing forests and wildlife as the bill proposes. And where will it all stop? If tribals get ownership of a village say, in Melghat Tiger Reserve: where will their children go to school? Will they not want electricity? How about hospitals? Do they not have the right to better communication and roads to better medical facilities etc? Will we provide for these? If not, what happens to the 'historical injustice' that the government aims to rectify with this bill? If yes, will someone please understand that a forest does not remain a forest once such development takes over. It starts as a village, develops into a town that ultimately morphs into an urban center.

A cub needs his forest and a healthy prey base if he is to become a tiger, not a school.

Solutions have themselves become problems. The TTF has come up with some good recommendations, like combating poaching by strengthening protection and amending the criminal provisions of the Wildlife Protection Act, 1972. I would say it is flogging a dead horse, each successive committee — there have been many — has been making similar

Leopard skin seizure in Delhi

recommendations through the past decade, nothing, yet, has come of it. Worryingly, the TTF's key agenda is that tiger habitats be shared with people. Noted tiger expert Valmik Thapar, member of the TTF, rues that much of the report has focused on how to improve the life of the people inside protected areas rather than protecting tigers inside them. So self-defeating is the report that questions are being raised whether the TTF is for or against the tiger. The headline of the summary of the report quoted that 'the agenda is to save the tiger the Indian way, where forests are not wilderness but habitats of people'. Come again? Isn't wilderness intrinsic to the very definition of forests?

Conservationists are not anti-people. One must recognise, too, that this is not a people vs tiger battle. Tribals must be given their rights but the quality of life they deserve cannot be administered within a reserve. The tiger is a symbol of our forests and our ecological and water security, tiger habitats form catchments of over 300 of India's important rivers. If we are to save the tiger, the minuscule land we have reserved for it must be inviolate. The one requirement for a tiger to thrive — as many examples show — are undistributed habitats.

Co-existence only sharpens conflicts between people and tiger. Let's understand this through the example of Melghat, once one of the finest tiger habitats, now degraded almost without redemption. Melghat has a pressure of more than one lakh cattle grazing within the sanctuary, killing the regeneration of the forest. There are 58 villages inside the reserve with a population of about 25,000 people, tribals included. But there is no cozy bonhomie with the animals. Wild boar, cheetal and other ungulates devastate crops, so in retaliation the people trap the animals and poison waterholes. Such methods do not kill discriminately, tigers

The KING and I

succumb as well. A forest guard who went to the waterhole to quench his thirst nearly died too, by the pesticides locals had sprayed inside. Booking offences has become increasingly problematic, with villagers threatening to set the forest on fire. It isn't an empty threat. Through the summer of 2005, forest guards fought raging fires, most falling critically ill while doing so. Locals also set the grasses on fire since the *tendu* leaves that they collect, flourishes if the grasses beneath are burnt.

Some miles away, as the crow flies, two tigers were poisoned last year at the edge of the Pench Tiger Reserve. In recent years there have been twenty cases of tiger poisoning in Nagarjunsagar in Andhra Pradesh. One can cite a hundred cases of such conflict. Ranthambhore, Bandhavgarh, Panna. And of course Sariska, the worst example of how a park is used, and abused, by wildlife traders to kill resident wildlife. The CBI report on Sariska confirmed this. The locals aren't mourning their losses either, just days after it was declared that there were no tigers in Sariska, thousands of people were on the streets demanding the denotification of the reserve, so that the mining lobby could move in, unhindered by 'nonsensical' forest laws.

Such conflicts are bound to get worse as protected areas get increasingly fragmented and become tiny islands pressed in by burgeoning human populations. Each tiger needs about fifty animals annually to survive and if we are to allow people and cows to share living space of the tiger, the conflict will be eternal and perennial. The tiger will lose out, always. Sariksa

made it to the headlines, in other forests, the tiger has died unsung. The tiger has lost over ninety-five per cent of its former range and the list is growing even post Sariska. Kela Devi and Sawai Man Singh sanctuary in Rajasthan, Palpur Kuno in Madhya Pradesh to name just a few.

A cozy co-existence between man and tiger is possible only in Utopia, not in reality, not in India. Forests are being used by insurrectionists and terrorists of all persuasions as a hiding place and a source of funding. Veerappan used sandalwood to finance his support from the Tamil Tigers from Sri Lanka. The People's War Group in Andhra Pradesh uses *katha*, raw material for a tobacco addictive to finance its armies that will continue to have an unlimited supply of guns and land mines so long as they can turn our unprotected forests to cash. In other words, our forests are financing the internal de-stabilisation of India.

The KING and I

Road kill, Kaziranga

How many tigers survive in India? The official figure quotes 3,750. Cynics call that a joke, cutting the figure down to 2,000 at best, probably even lesser. I wouldn't wager on either. The real answer is, no one knows. Figures are inflated, there is a battle on about the method of counting tigers, and so the numbers game continues. The only certainty is that few remain, and the numbers are declining further.

So, will the tiger survive this crisis? I will say yes, but maybe that's because I want to believe in it so desperately. I will be positive because I do not want to live in a world without tigers and all the other animals that make his kingdom. It must be yes, because the truth of the matter is if the tiger dies, we shall follow soon after.

And can it be saved? Only if we make a total commitment and take on the real battle: against an indifferent political system, the poachers and industrialists and miners whose only interest is to exploit the tiger's habitat. I fear that the tiger has become a victim of its popularity. He is the star on show for tourists in tiger reserves, translating into big money for tour operators. For most, the tiger is nothing but a cash cow, evident from hordes of tourist cars which chase the hapless beast in reserves, flouting every rule in the book. He is the main magnet to attract funds. A study by an independent UK-based agency shows that there are 550 NGOs in Delhi alone working to save the tiger. What work they do and where the money goes is a pertinent question.

Another study showed the huge funding poured into 'saving the tiger' is mismatched with the quantum of work, also citing specific examples of a few well-known and some not-so well-known NGOs. As for the forest department, it has its share of bad eggs. There are good officers too, but more often than not they are rarely allowed to function. In most cases those totally unacquainted with wildlife management are put in charge of parks and reserves and entrusted with wildlife work.

A classic example is the former chief wildlife warden of Rajasthan who, when confronted with the current Sariska-Ranthambhore disaster, announced his grand plan to save the tiger: 'We must save the tigers the way South Africa is doing it: they increased the population from two to eight.' Someone should educate the man who holds (he has been replaced since then) the highest wildlife post in his state that these two tigers were raised in captivity in the US and now thrive in semi-captive conditions, and are handfed their daily bread. South Africa has never in its history had wild tigers. Is it any wonder that with such people at the helm, the obituary of all the major protected areas of Rajasthan – Sariska, Ranthambhore and Bharatpur – is all but written?

Getting over the present calamity is a monumental task, but given the will it can be done. First we must decide whether we want to save the tiger, if yes, how many, and where. Then pick up the most viable places. Like Kanha, Kaziranga and Corbett that have minimum human pressure. The Bandipur-Nagarhole-Madumalai-Wayanad belt in the south is another example.

Empower Project Tiger, and bring the disjointed reserves under one umbrella, not subject to the varying whims of wayward state governments. At the same time, make the states

Park management in Ranthambhore

The KING and I

accountable for 'their' tigers. Split the Ministry of Environment and Forests, with one arm looking at urban pollution and the other devoted to wildlife. Create a separate wildlife service, well-trained and staffed to combat poaching, properly versed in wildlife management. Inject life in the comatose Wildlife Crime Bureau. Take assistance of the police and national and international investigative agencies to break the back of organised wildlife crime and prepare a well-armed, well-trained cadre of forest police. Foresters must be given immunity, like the police, in encounters with poachers, and para-military forces should be deployed in reserves. NGOs must join hands to direct funding towards equipping forest service, strengthening infrastructure for better management. The protected area network – which is just four per cent of India – must be made inviolate. The world's most charismatic animal is fairly adaptable to its changing environs and a prolific breeder, if undisturbed. Give it wild spaces, protect it fiercely and the tiger will thrive.

Nor can India battle alone. If the hunger for tiger bones and furs does not cease on foreign shores, the king of beasts will always live under the shadow of the gun.

All this is a tall order, almost an impossible dream, but if at all we are to save the tiger then dream we must. India has for years led other countries in conservation. Let us not lose our national heritage to petty, immediate concerns. Let us not lose the tiger for want of a collective effort. Let us not rob the tiger of its future.

Afterword

So much has happened since this book began, since I begin visiting wild India and getting involved with India's wildlife and the threats it faces.

The year 2004-2005 put an end to the farce that we are leading the world in conserving tigers. The tiger, and India's varied wildlife, is vanishing. Fast. The tiger is extinct in Sariska, Palpur Kuno, Keladevi. In other reserves and protected areas, their numbers are falling drastically. The obvious killer is the poacher and the trader, local people who speared the tiger in Sariska and Sansar Chand who reached the skin and bones to the buyer in China and the Far East. But there are other killers who don benign masks; politicians who are selling tiger habitat for votes and other gains, industrialists and miners who destroy habitats, bureaucrats and officials who wear blinkers in the face of a crisis, NGOs who have made the tiger their business, and, we, the people, who do not care whether the tiger lives. Or dies.

On a more personal level, the most painful part of writing this book is the loss of the protagonists. Tigers and other animals, killed by the poacher's gun. The Bakula tigress in Ranthambhore, who fell asleep in front of my jeep, is gone. Presumed dead. As is 113, 'my' tigress in Panna. She has disappeared, killed, most likely. A poacher caught by the police in Chattarpur, close to Panna, confessed to having employed local tribals to kill tigers and other animals. He has sold in the recent past five tiger and thirty leopard skins, plus forty kilos of tiger bones to the kingpin of the trade, Sansar Chand.

Was that lovely tigress I met, 113 among them? I weep when I think of the immense joy these cats gave me. I am ashamed when I think of the faith the tigers had in human beings, their ability to kill yet refraining from doing so. I had interrupted 113's meal, yet she left me unharmed, the Bakula tigress and her three cubs, almost full grown tigers, had surrounded our jeep but never for a moment did I sense real danger. Who, may I ask, among us is the beast here, and who is civilised? The answer is obvious. I did not personally set the trap or point the gun, but I feel the guilt and the burden. I, we, betrayed the tiger.

Acknowledgements

My first, and deepest, gratitude is for all the denizens of the forest, who have given me much happiness in life.

This book owes a debt to many people, both past and present but a special word of thanks should go to Rajan Mehra of Rupa and Co. who first approached me with the idea of doing a book, based on my travels in Tigerland. I would like to specially thank my long-suffering editor of *Darpan* and *The Pioneer*, Chandan Mitra, who took my unending request for travel into the wilds with his usual grace and more importantly, gave the tiger a habitat in newsprint. If he did not believe in me, this book would never have been written.

Ashok Kumar, should I thank you, or otherwise, for introducing me to the wild world, and ensuring that I never wavered. Fatji, the ultimate tiger teacher, Bittu Sahgal, who gave me my first 'wild' job, P. K. Sen for his motivation, Valmik Thapar, whose books were an inspiration, Belinda Wright, a great source of information, George Schaller, for being so generous with his time. Billy Arjan Singh, for the battles you fight and for being a kind host. Mike Pandey and Vivek Menon for their encouragement. Kishore Rithe, for his unstinting devotion to the wilds. Thank you, all you 'Tiger People' with whom I have spent many precious hours discussing the plight of the tiger and who now have their work cut out. More power to them. Bikram Grewal, friend and part-time foe, used his considerable experience to ensure the book saw the light of day. With what words do I thank thee?

My search for photographs came to an end when the veteran photographers Vivek Sinha, N. C. Dhingra and Niranjan Sant opened their archives and allowed me unlimited access to their lifetimes work. My debt to them is immeasurable. Equal generosity was shown by Otto Pfister, Sumit Sen, Clement Francis M, Mukesh Acharya, Bhushan Pandya, Kalyan Varma, Yathin S. K., Sujan, Koustabh, Bhaskar, Nautambhai Dave. I am beholden to all of you. Ravi Vyas, Disha and Neeraj Aggarwal helped with the editing and designing of the book.

Dr. Rajesh Gopal and Sanjeev Chadda, for their immense help and faith. P. R. Sinha, Sandeep Kumar, and many others from the Ministry of Environment and Forests gave me both moral and logistic support. I would like in particular to thank S. C. Sharma, H. S. Singh,

Acknowledgements

S. K. Chakravorthy, Bharat Pathak, C. M. Seth, Nitin Kakodkar, Shri Bhagwan, A. R. Bharti, Shekhar Neeraj, Girish Vashisht, Santosh Tewary, Shafat Hussein, G. S. Bhardwaj, D. M. Shukla, Shyamal Tikedar, Ritesh Bhattacharjee, R. Modi, Khageshwar Naik, Digvijay Singh Khatti, Samir Sinha, P. P. Raval, Ramanuj Choudhary, R. N. Mehrotra, Ashok Badaik, Y. K. Das, G. S. Pande, A. N. Prasad, V. P. Singh, and the late Ashok Kumar. My eternal gratitude to the foresters, guards, trackers, mahouts, guides, our precious and unsung green army. They are all brave warriors and had it not been for them the subject of this book would have disappeared much earlier. My thanks to the staff of the various forest resthouses I have stayed in, and whose luxuriant hospitality matches none. Good company in the field made it all the more enjoyable and I had the happy opportunity of meeting many people on my various journeys. Some now have become friends and include Mark Shand, Avni Patel, Mohit Aggarwal, Nanu, Visha, Pratap, Shruti, Rinchen, Gopi Sundar, Vinny, Pankaj Chandan, Mark Davidar, Aditya, Asit, Abhra, A. Das. Thank you all for your hospitality and friendship.

Kam, my forever friend, you were the one who set me on this path and taught me the power of words. Thank you so, for pushing me on when I was ready to give up. To my not-so-wild friends for being there, always; Bhavna, Geeta, Geetu, Sandy, Sujoy, Meghna, Manoj, Gauri, Dr. Sangeeta, Lata, Ashish, Anni, Kandharp, Gautam, Neha and Julie. I am grateful to Aruna, Malati, Tejal, Devjibhai who made life easier. Sheila Masi, for giving me a home in Delhi. Ditto Bobby, Neelu and the kids. Mamaji, for your affection. Madhu Sahgal for being so caring in difficult times. To the *Darpan* and *Pioneer* team, notably Rinku for her patience each time I ditched the horrors of production and escaped into wilderness. Ashok Sharma, for bailing me out, unfailingly, when stranded in numerous airports.

Ours has always been a very close family and had it has not been for their support, I would have never trod upon my chosen path. My father, J. S. Bindra has always encouraged my unusual interest in the wilds, even if it meant keeping his counsel. Thanks for being there, Papa. I have — no arguments here — the best brother in the world. Thanks, Jaspreet, for everything. Frooti, Snoopi and my numerous canine friends, who taught me to love animals. Yes, Uncle Max, I can see your hurt look, you had a 'paw' in this, too. The greatest support in my life is my mother, whose love and caring for me can never be repaid in several lifetimes. This one is for you, Ma.

Photo-credits

Alwin Singh: 144/145, 147, 148, 150b, 151, 152a, 211a
Amano Samarpan: 80/81, 166/167, 250/251
Bikram Grewal: cover, back flap, 27, 30a, 30b, 56, 57a, 57b, 58a, 168, 198/199, 202, 206, 207, 211b, 213a, 213b, 220/221, 222, 223, 234, 235, 236, 240
Billy Arjan Singh: (courtesy) 34, 35, 36a, 36b, 39b,
Bhushan Pandya: 94a, 94b, 94c
Clement M Francis: 28, 70a, 106/107, 116b, 132/133, 228
Dipankar Ghosh: 11
D. K. Bhaskar: 120/121, 124/125, 128
Fateh Singh Rathore: Front Flap, 18a, 21, Courtesy 14a, 73
Forest Dept. Jammu & Kashmir: 150a
Gajendra Singh: 110/111
Jagdish Yadav: 142
Jennifer Buxton: 161
Kalyan Varma: 69
Kishor Rithe: 61, 100, 101
Koustabh Sharma: 156/157
Mark Davidar: 179, 182b
Mukesh Acharya: 10, 90/91, 96, 97
N. A. Naseer: 180
N. C. Dhingra: back cover, endpapers, 3, 7, 18b, 20/21, 22/23, 28, 38/39, 42/43, 66/67, 68, 76/77, 104, 108, 114, 130/131, 154/155, 158, 159, 169, 176/177, 181b, 191, 209, 212, 214a, 217, 218/219 247, 248
Nauthambhai K. Dave: 92a, 92b, 93a, 93b, 123a
Niranjan Sant: 4/5, 8, 52b, 71, 88/89, 95, 112a, 116a, 137, 139, 218/219, 226
Otto Pfister: 146, 149, 152b, 153a, 153b

Prerna Bindra: 14b, 15a, 15b, 26a, 26b, 38b, 49, 58b, 64, 65, 70b, 72, 78/79, 84, 87a, 87b, 109, 122a, 123b, 134, 135, 138, 140, 170a, 170b, 171, 172,173, 174, 175, 181a, 184a, 184b, 195b, 214b, 215a, 215b, 216, 225a, 225b, 227, 229b, 249, 256
Sanctuary: 60 (Bittu Saghal), 103 (Rohit Vyas), 117b (Debal Sen), 127, 203 (Vivek Sinha), 238/239 (Anish Andheria)
Sumit Sen: 9, 24/25, 59, 86, 105, 188
Sujan Chatterjee: 44/45, 46, 48, 50b, 52a, 53, 54/55, 58c, 62/63, 83, 85
Teki Tanwar: 47, 50a, 51
Toby Sinclair: 32/33, 37, 40, 41, 201
Uttaranchal Forest Dept.: 126a, 126b
Valmik Thapar: 1, 16/17, 164/165, 195a
Yathin S. K.: 117a
Vivek Sinha: 2, 6, 12/13, 19, 74/75, 98/99, 102, 112b, 113, 115, 118/119, 122b, 136, 141, 143, 160, 162, 163, 178, 182a, 183, 185, 186/187, 190, 192, 193, 194, 196, 197, 204/205, 208, 210, 224, 232/233
Wildlife Institute of India: 29, 31
Wildlife Protection Society of India: 229a, 230/231, 245a 245b, 246
Wildlife Trust of India: 237, 241, 242, 243, 244

The publishers and the author would like to express their appreciation to the photographers for kindly permitting the use of their work. Every effort has been made to correctly identify the copyright holders of the photographs. However in the case of any discrepancy, the photographers should approach the author for correction in subsequent editions.

Bibliography

Ahmad, S: Charger, *The Long Living Tiger*, Allahabad, 2001
Alter, S: *Elephus Maximus*, Delhi, 2004
Ali, S: *The Fall of a Sparrow*, Delhi, 1985
Anderson, K: *This is the Jungle: More Tales of Man-eaters*, London, 1964
Anderson, K: *Nine Man-eaters and a Rouge*, London, 1955
Anderson, K: *Man-eaters and Jungle Killers*, London, 1959
Baldwin, J: *The Large and Small Game of Bengal and NW Provinces of India*, London, 1877
Barnes, S: *Tiger*, London, 1994
Baze, W: *Tiger, Tiger*, London, 1957
Bedi, R & Bedi, R: *Indian Wildlife*, Delhi, 1884
Bedi, R: *India's Wild Wonders*, Delhi, 1991
Best, J: *Forest Life in India*, London, 1935
Bhaskaran, T: *The Dance of the Sarus*, Delhi, 1999
Booth, M: *Carpet Sahib*, Delhi, 1986
Braddon, E: *Thirty Years of Shikar*, London, 1895
Brandar, D: *Wild Animals of Central India*, London, 1923
Brunskill, C: *Tiger Forest*, London, 2004
Burton, R: *The Tiger Hunters*, Delhi, Reprint, 2002
Chakrabarti, K: *Man-Eating Tigers*, Calcutta, 1992
Champion, F: *With a Camera in Tigerland*, London, 1935
Champion, F: *The Jungle in Sunlight and Shadow*, London, 1934
Chaodhary, S: *Khairi: Beloved Tigress*, Dehradun, 1999
Corbett, J: *Man-Eaters of Kumaon*, London, 1946
Corbett, J: *The Temple Tiger*, London, 1955
Corbett, J: *The Man-eating Leopard of Rudraprayag*, London, 1947
Courtney, N: *The Tiger-Symbol of Freedom*, London, 1980
Cubitt, G: *Wild India*, London, 1985
Daniel, J: (ed) *A Century of Natural History*, Mumbai, 1986
Daniel, J: (ed) *The Leopard in India*, Dehradun, 1996
Daniel, J: (ed) *The Tiger In India*, Dehradun, 2001
Davidar, E: *Cheetal Walk*, Delhi, 1997
Dharmakumarsinh, R: *Reminiscences of Indian Wildlife*, Delhi, 1998
Divyabhanusing: *The End of Trail-The Cheetah in India*, Delhi, 1996
Divyabhanusing: *The Story of Asia's Lions*, Mumbai, 2005
Dwivedi, S & Allen, C: *Lives of the Indian Princes*, London, 1984
Fayrer, J: *Royal Tiger of Bengal*, 1875
Forbes, J: *Wanderings of a Naturalist*
Forsyth, J: *Highlands of Central India*, London, 1879
Gee, E: *The Wildlife of India*, London, 1964
Ghorpade, M: *Sunlight and Shadows*, London, 1983
Grewal, B: (ed) *Indian Wildlife*, Singapore, 1997
Grewal, B: *Birds of India*, London, 2004

Guha, R: (ed) *Nature's Spokesman*, M Krishnan, Delhi, 2000
Gurung, K: *Mammals of India*, Delhi, 1996
Hammond, N: *Artists for Nature-India*, 2000
Hanley, P: *Tiger Trails in Assam*, London, 1961
Hillard, D: *Vanishing Tracks-Four Years amongst Snow Leopards*, London, 1989
Hornocker, M: *Track of the Tiger*, New York, 1997
Jackson, P: *Endangered Species: Tigers*, London, 1990
Jaleel, J: *Under the Shadows of Man-Eaters*, Canada, 1997
Jerdon, T: *The Mammals of India*, London, 1867
Johnsingh, A: *On Corbett's Trail*. Delhi, 2004
Karanth, U: *The Way of the Tiger*, Bangalore, 2002
Kipling, R: *The Jungle Book*, 1894
Krishnan, M: *Jungle and Backyard*, Delhi, 1961
Krishnan, M: *Night and Days*, Delhi, 1985
Kumar, A & Menon, V: *Wildlife Crime*, Delhi, 1998
Lahiri-Chaudhary, D: *The Great Indian Elephant Book*, Delhi, 2000
Manfredi, P: (ed) *In Danger*, Delhi, 1997
Matthiessen, P: *The Snow Leopard*, London, 1979
McDougal, C: *Face of the Tiger*, London, 1977
McNeelay, et al: *The Soul of the Tiger*, New York, 1988
Menon, V: *A Field-guide to the Mammals of India*, Delhi, 2003
Monga, S: *Wildlife Reserves of India*, Mumbai, 2003
Montgomery, S: *Spell of the Tiger*, Delhi, 2002
Mountford, G: *Tigers*, Newton Abbot, 1973
Mountford, G: *Back From the Brink*, London, 1978
Mountford, G: *Saving the Tiger*, London, 1981
Musselwhite, A: *Behind the Lens in Tigerland*, London, 1933
Niyogi, T: *Tiger: Cult of the Sunderbans*, Kolkata, 1933
Naidu, M: *Trail of the Tiger*, Dehradun, 1998
Osborne, M: *Tigers at Twilight*, London, 1999
Panwar, H: *Kanha National Park*, Ahmedabad, 1991
Perry, R: *The World of the Tiger*, London, 1964
Prater, S: *The Book of Indian Animals*, Mumbai, 1988
Pye-Smith, C: *In Search of Wild India*, London, 1993
Rangarajan, M: *The Oxford Anthology of Indian Wildlife Vols. 1 & 2*, Delhi, 1999
Ranjitsinh, M: *Beyond the Tiger*, Delhi, 1997
Rice, W: *Tiger Shooting in India*, London, 1854
Roberts, TJ: *Mammals of Pakistan*, London, 1977
Saharia, V: *Wildlife in India*, Dehradun, 1982
Sanderson, G: *Thirteen Years amongst the Beasts of India*, London, 1878
Sankhala, K: *Tigress*, London, 1978
Schaller, G: *Mountain Monarchs*, Chicago, 1977
Schaller, G: *The Deer and the Tiger*, London, Chicago, 1967
Schaller, G: *The Stones of Silence*, London, 1980
Scott, J: *The Leopard's Tale*, London, 1985
Seidensticker, J: *Tiger*, Cambridge, 1996

Seidensticker, J et al: *Riding the Tiger*, Cambridge, 1999
Shah, A: *A Tiger's Tale*, Kingston, 1996
Shahi, S: *Back to the Wall*. Delhi, 1977
Sharma, B: *High Altitude Wildlife in India*, Delhi, 1994
Sharma, H: *Ranthambhore Sanctuary*, Delhi, 2002
Sheshadri, D: *The Twilight of India's Wildlife*, London, 1969
Sukhla, R: *Leopards in the Backyard*, Delhi, 2002
Singh, A: *The Legend of the Man-Eater*, Delhi, 1993
Singh, A: *Tiger Haven*, London, 1973
Singh, A: *Tara, A tigress*, London, 1891
Singh, A: *Tiger! Tiger!*, London, 1984
Singh, A: *Eelie and the Big Cats*, Delhi, 2001
Singh, A: *Tiger Book*, Delhi, 1997
Singh, A: *Prince of Cats*, Delhi, 2001
Singh, A: *Watching India's Wildlife*, Delhi, 2004
Singh, K: *The Tiger of Rajasthan*, London, 1959
Singh, K: *Hints on Tiger Shooting*, Mumbai, 1969
Singh, K: *One Man and a Thousand Tigers*, New York, 1959
Sinha, V: *The Vanishing Tiger*, London, 2003
Srivastava, A: *Asiatic Lion on the Brink*, Dehradun, 1999
Stacey, P: *Tigers*, London, 1968
Sterndale, A: *A Natural History of the Mammalia of India*, Dehradun, Reprint, 1982
Sukumar, S: *Elephant Days and Nights*, Delhi, 1994
Sunquist, F & M: *Tiger Moon*, Chicago, 1988
Thapar, V & Singh, F: *With Tigers in the Wild*, New Delhi, 1983
Thapar, V: *The Tigers Destiny*, London, 1995
Thapar, V: *Tiger-Portrait of a Predator*, London, 1986
Thapar, V: *The Secret Life of the Tigers*, Delhi, 1989
Thapar, V: *Land of the Tiger*, London, 1998
Thapar, V & Singh, F: *Wild Tigers of Ranthambore*, Delhi, 2000
Thapar, V: Tigers: *Habitats, Life Cycle, Threats*, London, 1999
Thapar, V: Tiger: *The Ultimate Guide*, 2004
Thapar, V: *Cult of the Tiger*, Delhi, 2002
Thapar, V: *Battling for Survival*, Delhi, 2003
Tilson, R: *Tigers of the World*, New Jersey, 1987
Toovey, J: (ed) *Tigers of the Raj*, Gloucester, 1987
Tritsch, M: *Wildlife of India*, London, 2001
Tyabji, H: *Bandavgarh*, Delhi, 1994
Ward, G & R: *Tiger wallahs*, New York, 1993
Ward, G: *The Year of the Tiger*, Washington, 1998
Wright, B & Breedon S: *Through the Tiger's Eye*, Berkley, 1996
WWF Nepal: *The Snow Leopard Manual*, Kathmandu, 2002
Zwaeanpoel, J: *Tigers*, San Francisco, 1992

The KING and I

Always secretive
Never devious
Always a killer
Never a murderer
Solitary
Never alone

- John Seidensticker